100 BEST IDEAS

to **turbocharge** *your*

children's ministry

Dale Hudson & Scott Werner

Group

Group resources really work!

This Group resource incorporates our R.E.A.L. approach to ministry. It reinforces a growing friendship with Jesus, encourages long-term learning, and results in life transformation, because it's

Relational
Learner-to-learner interaction enhances learning and builds Christian friendships.

Experiential
What learners experience through discussion and action sticks with them up to 9 times longer than what they simply hear or read.

Applicable
The aim of Christian education is to equip learners to be both hearers and doers of God's Word.

Learner-based
Learners understand and retain more when the learning process takes into consideration how they learn best.

Group

100 Best Ideas to Turbocharge Your Children's Ministry
Copyright © 2013 Dale Hudson and Scott Werner

Visit our website: **group.com**

Credits
Patty Anderson, Pam Clifford, Andrea Filer, Dale Hudson, Jan Kershner, DeAnne Lear, Joani Schultz, Dena Twinem, Scott Werner, Matt Wood, Christine Yount Jones
Print Production Artist: PerfecType, Nashville, TN

Unless otherwise indicated, all Scripture quotations are taken from the *Holy Bible*, New Living Translation, copyright © 1996, 2004. Used by permission of Tyndale House Publishers, Inc., Carol Stream, Illinois 60188. All rights reserved.

Library of Congress Cataloging-in-Publication Data
Hudson, Dale, 1967-
  100 best ideas to turbocharge your children's ministry / [Dale Hudson and Scott Werner].
    p. cm.
  Rev. ed. of: Turbocharged!, 100 simple secrets to successful children's ministry.
  ISBN 978-0-7644-9853-4 (pbk.)
  1. Church work with children. I. Werner, Scott A., 1968- II. Hudson, Dale, 1967- Turbocharged!, 100 simple secrets to successful children's ministry. III. Title.
  BV639.C4H79 2013
  259'.22—dc23
                              2012036626

Printed in the United States of America.
10 9 8 7 6 5 4 3   22 21 20 19 18 17 16 15 14

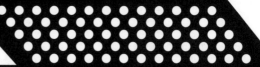

CONTENTS

FOREWORD

As a parent, there is nothing I'm more excited about than proven tools that will help my kids know and love Jesus. That is part of the reason I'm so thankful for Dale, Scott, and *100 Best Ideas to Turbocharge Your Children's Ministry*. I've seen first-hand how these ideas can impact a child's life…and a parent's.

As a pastor, I've also seen the incredible energy a dynamic children's ministry can bring into the life of a church. People say children are the future, but they are also the present. Ministries and churches that thrive tomorrow are those impassioned about kids today. When a child grows in his or her faith, the whole family wins. We've seen many children literally bring their parents to church and to faith. That's why I believe these ideas can rescue families and renew churches.

Dale and Scott are two individuals with loads of experience and proven ways to help kids and parents grow and learn. These teachings really can make an eternal difference in the life of a person and a church. I, for one, am thankful for the difference they have made in my family and in our church.

—Jud Wilhite, author of *Stripped: Uncensored Grace on the Streets of Vegas*
and senior pastor of Central Christian Church, Las Vegas

DEDICATIONS

To Pamela, my life was made complete when God brought us together. Your sweet spirit endears me…your beauty makes my heart beat faster. Thanks for always being there. I look forward to spending the rest of my life with you. I love you.

To Josh and Caleb, my two sons, I am so proud of you. You are growing each day into men of God. God has awesome plans for you. I can't wait to see what he does with your lives in the years ahead. I love you.

To Van and Sandy Hudson, my parents, you've always been an anchor in my life. Your passion for following Christ is my greatest example. I love you.

To all the incredible people I have served with in children's ministry. Thanks for giving your life to what matters most. Your impact will be felt for generations to come and throughout eternity.

—Dale

Special thanks and dedication to:

My bride and best friend—Tammy—for believing in me every step of the way.

My sons—Dustin, Dillon, and Braden—for showing me how to be a Dad.

My Pastor—Groesch—for standing on the mountaintop.

I love you all dearly.

—Scott

Would you like to *turbocharge* your children's ministry? To see it propelled forward with new passion and vision, operating at a higher level of effectiveness?

If the answer is *yes,* then you've picked up the right resource. This book was born from the desire to see children's ministries everywhere make a difference in their communities. We've leaned on 29 years of combined ministry experience to bring you the best ideas, practices, and philosophies to energize *your* ministry.

Our ideas didn't come from just "talking" about ministry, but from frontline, hands-on experience. Over the years, we've seen these practices bring great spiritual and numerical growth in the ministries we have led. We believe they can do the same for you.

Our prayer is that senior pastors who read this book will be reminded of the importance of children's ministry in their churches. For children's pastors and directors, we hope to create a burning desire for next-level ministry. And for volunteers, here are tested ways to transform your program.

Let's be honest, though. Turbocharged ministry is risky. It will move you out of your comfort zone. It may mean some ministry engine overhauling. You may wonder if making the switch to turbocharged ministry is really worth it. We would say *yes*…a thousand rpm over!

The countdown clock is ticking on our opportunity to make a difference. We must reach kids while their hearts are still open to the things of God. We must reach out to families and offer them hope before many of them disintegrate. The kids and families in your city need a turbocharged children's ministry!

May God use this book to turbocharge you and your ministry!

One of my favorite television shows is *The First 48* on the A&E channel. It's a real-life documentary that places you right in the middle of a murder investigation. You're there when the murder report is first received, and you journey with the detective through the next 48 hours as he or she tries to solve the crime. As soon as the murder call has been received, the clock starts ticking down from 48 hours, because if the detective doesn't get a lead in the first 48 hours, the chances of solving the crime are cut in half.

There is another clock that ticks down each week. It's an unseen clock at your church or ministry. When a new family drives in, you have 8 minutes to make a good impression. If you don't maximize those first 8 minutes, the chances of the family returning goes down. So grab your investigative gear. A new family has just driven onto your church property. You've got 8 minutes, and the clock just started ticking.

8 minutes and ticking. The parking lot is full. The family is wondering if they will ever find a place to park. Suddenly they see empty parking spaces right up front. The spaces are marked "First-Time Guests." They feel relieved—and valued!

IDEAS

- Reserve and mark front spaces for guests.
- Trying to reach young families with preschoolers? Reserve parking spots close to the building that say "Preschool Family Parking." The mom who has to carry a baby, diaper bag, and corral a toddler or two will thank you and be back.
- Take it to the next level by offering valet parking for moms with little ones.

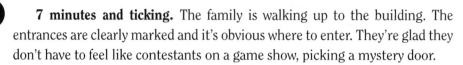

7 minutes and ticking. The family is walking up to the building. The entrances are clearly marked and it's obvious where to enter. They're glad they don't have to feel like contestants on a game show, picking a mystery door.

IDEAS

- Identify entrances and key buildings with signs on the outside.
- Take it to the next level by having parking lot attendants and hosts who can help families know where to go even before they approach the building.

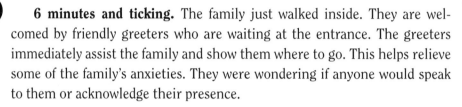

6 minutes and ticking. The family just walked inside. They are welcomed by friendly greeters who are waiting at the entrance. The greeters immediately assist the family and show them where to go. This helps relieve some of the family's anxieties. They were wondering if anyone would speak to them or acknowledge their presence.

IDEAS

- Have trained, friendly greeters at each entrance door. They should be identified with a shirt, badge, or name tag that shows they're greeters.
- Train greeters to watch for first-time families. They are the ones that look unsure…you know…the deer-in-the-headlights look.

5 minutes and ticking. The family is escorted to a check-in area reserved for first-time families. Here they are met by a first-time-family host. The host helps them check in and gives the parents vital information about the children's environments. The host then personally walks the family to the children's rooms.

IDEAS

- Have a check-in area that is just for first-time families. Never make them get in line with your regular members or attendees.
- Train a team of first-time-family hosts. Have them clearly communicate vital information about the check-in process, security, and checkout, but don't overwhelm parents with too much information.
- Keep your hosts informed of current information and events so they can answer any questions the family may have.

- Give first-time parents a pager for their children (elementary included). This is one of the best things you can do to make parents feel at ease. Reassure the parents that you will page them immediately if any issues arise.

- Each first-time child should receive a name tag. This allows leaders and other kids in the room to welcome the new child. If all children wear name tags (which is highly recommended), give a first-time child a special sticker to put on his or hers.

3 minutes and ticking. The host escorts the family to the children's area. Greeters welcome the kids and parents. The kids are immediately paired with other kids who are waiting to make them feel welcome and at ease. The parents are invited to look inside the room and are given a brief explanation of what their children will experience. They are also given clear pickup instructions again. A few key leaders come over to greet the new family and reassure them that the kids are in for a great experience. The parents are still a little apprehensive about leaving their kids, but feel more at ease because of the care they have been shown.

IDEAS

- Enlist and train a team of children who will welcome new children. They pair up with new children and stay with them for the entire experience. Pair boys with boys and girls with girls.

- It's vital to have a great team of adult leaders in place. Follow proper adult-child ratios. Nothing will make a new family more apprehensive than seeing a room full of kids with not enough adult leaders. But when parents walk in a room and see enough competent, trained, and enthusiastic leaders, it speaks volumes to them. You can be sure new families are making this assessment whether they are vocal about it or not.

30 seconds and ticking. The parents are escorted by the host to the worship area. They are met by greeters who welcome them and help them find a seat.

IDEAS

- Hosts should walk parents all the way to the auditorium or adult classroom. Don't leave them hanging after they get their kids situated.

- Take it to the next level by having hosts meet the parents again after the service to assist them in checking their kids out.

Time is up. The family has been treated with courtesy and professionalism. The first 8 minutes have not been without anxiety, but the family has felt cared for and valued.

This weekend a new family will pull into your parking lot. Perhaps they're new to town. Perhaps they don't attend church but have decided to give this "God thing" one shot. Whatever the story, they will arrive, and their first 8 minutes will make an impression on them. We're praying that God will use those 8 minutes to make an eternal impact on their lives!

—**Dale**

A Fine's Not Fine

> "Choose a good reputation over great riches; being held in high esteem is better than silver or gold."
>
> —Proverbs 22:1

I used to hate copyrights. Too strong? It's true. For years, every time I turned around, someone was telling me *no*. "No! You can't use that movie clip." "No! You can't have a video in the background during worship." "No! You can't use that song on your teaching DVD." "No! Bad children's pastor!" (OK, that last one may be an exaggeration.) It was a source of constant frustration, shackling my creativity and artistic vision. "Why don't they understand?" I fumed. "I just want to engage these kids so I can share Christ with them!"

Then I became friends with a few artists. Gradually, the reality they lived began to dawn on me. What if every product I ever slaved over, someone else took from me, without asking, without paying me for it? I have a family to feed. If someone did that to me, that would be wrong. Ouch.

Rise to the challenge. When, for whatever reason, you can't acquire the rights to a piece to support your message or enhance your presentation, you have to dig deep. You have to create it yourself, or use the talent that God has placed all around you. I realized that, many times, using someone else's work was more of an easy out than the best option. Don't misunderstand me. We knew that we couldn't compete with the expertise, the craftsmanship that professionals could deliver. But we had many things they didn't: us, locations familiar to our audiences, personalized greetings, and beloved characters. Over time, as our commitment increased, so did our abilities, which also increased our quality. Our dedication to our true craft—which was not elaborate video production, but drawing kids toward Christ—led us to start from scratch when we would plan a series. We'd ask ourselves, "What can *we* do?" I'd argue that God honored that commitment.

—**Scott**

Transition: Building a Bridge

When kids need to transition to a new ministry environment, it can be a scary time for them *and* their parents. But a strategic plan can turn transition into a time of anticipation, excitement, and spiritual growth for the kids and families in your ministry. Here are some ways to build an effective bridge during transition.

Create a partnership between environments. Helping environments work together is key to building the bridge.

IDEA

- Have key staff from the new environment come and meet the transitioning kids. Have them hang out before a service, greet the kids from the stage, or even teach a lesson. We start this process three months before transition. The key staff members come at least twice a month.

Communicate. Send out communication pieces to parents. Start communicating about transition at least two months out.

IDEAS

- Send a welcome packet to parents of transitioning kids. Include a welcome letter, sample lessons, sample take-home papers, a calendar with important dates, sign-up forms, and any other pertinent information parents will want to know.

- Announce the transition to the kids. Make it fun and exciting. Tell them about cool things that will be coming up in the new environment.

- Take the kids to their new environment and give them a preview before they transition. This will relieve a lot of anxiety as kids see the environment and get a feel for what it will be like.

- Have an open house. It's a great way for kids and parents to visit the new environment, ask questions, get information, and meet their new leaders. Have key staff in the room to meet the new kids and their parents. Have information packets available. And consider families' busy schedules. Consider offering several options for families to attend.

Have a graduation ceremony. Offer families a spiritual milestone they will never forget.

IDEAS

- Ask volunteers who have worked with the kids to share memories.
- Ask graduating kids to share what they've learned, memories, and thanks to their leaders.
- Ask parents to publicly bless their kids with Scripture, thoughts, and prayer. (Ask everyone ahead of time so they have time to prepare.)
- Provide graduation certificates or maybe even gifts.
- Have kids walk across the stage. This is visual confirmation that they are transitioning to a new environment.
- Give a brief devotion or challenge to the kids and parents. Then close with prayer. Let parents and leaders gather around the children and pray for them.
- Have a party, cookout, or reception after the ceremony. This is a great time for staff, volunteers, and students from the new ministry environment to connect with transitioning kids and parents.

Keep kids grouped together as much as possible. Keeping groups together will provide security for kids and help them continue to deepen relationships.

Have volunteers move up with kids. We love it when volunteers want to move up with their kids! It helps calm kids' fears, but more important, when a leader invests in a child's life over the years, the spiritual impact is multiplied.

Make yourself available for kids or families who are struggling during transition. I have found over the years that transition has a way of revealing kids and families who need an extra ministry touch. Perhaps it brings out the anxiety a child may still be feeling from a divorce; perhaps it shows parenting challenges a mom or dad is facing. How will you know who they are?

Don't worry…usually they will come to you. Whatever the need, be there to encourage them and walk with them through this time.

One of the great joys of being in children's ministry for the long haul is seeing kids grow up and become fully devoted followers of Christ. It reminds you that all the time you spent building bridges for them was well worth it.

My son, Josh, is a senior in high school this year. It seems like just yesterday he was a little first-grader in children's worship. Now as I look up at him (he's 6'4"), I'm so proud. He loves God with all his heart. He has a bright future ahead of him as he follows Christ.

The kids in your ministry will grow up just as fast. Be there to build bridges across the transitions.

—**Dale**

What do you do for outreach? Maybe nothing. Maybe something every week. No matter how much you're currently involved in your community, you have the opportunity to reach past the walls of your building and into your community. If you need some help, partnering with your missions department is a great place to start. Find a food bank, visit a government housing complex, volunteer at your local children's hospital. Get out there. It will change your life.

Build it...*and* go. In the early years of our ministry, we were pretty self-absorbed. We weren't even trying to get outside our walls. Our church's approach brought the outside to us. We didn't *have* to go, because they were constantly coming to us. Reflecting on it today makes me sad.

Where did we get our *Field of Dreams* mentality? "If we build it, they will come." Jesus said simply, "Go." He said to feed the hungry, clothe the naked, and comfort the hurting. According to Jesus, it's not about growth. In fact, I imagine he'd rather we cut some resource-hogging meetings and programs and instead go to a hospital, visit a prison, or go to a homeless shelter.

As we wrestled with this issue over the years, Gina, one of my team members, began to inspire me. She leads one of our campuses that's equivalent in size to 10 other campuses combined. Gina's a star.

God burdened Gina's heart to reach out to her community. She had led her team in many different successful projects. Then she struck gold. Gina decided she wanted to build a relationship with the public school closest to her campus. In Oklahoma, schools rarely allow churches access because they're afraid of violating the separation of church and state. I have personally been declined access to have lunch with children from our ministry even when their parents requested it and gave their permission. But Gina's smarter than I am. Here's what she and her team have done:

- Provided snacks for the teachers lounge.
- Raised money to buy DVD players for classrooms.
- Volunteered at community events, such as sporting events and carnivals.
- Adopted a flower bed and organized work days to maintain it.
- Provided a volunteer base for the school's book fair.
- Provided backpacks and school supplies for kids in need.

Gina didn't just attend an event. She built a relationship. Her team has become a trusted partner to the school. She has gained access to kids who attend the school, and not just the ones who go to our church. We can all learn from Gina's example. It doesn't have to be a school. Maybe it's a benevolence ministry, or a special-needs facility, or a nursing home. Whatever it is, you can make a difference.

Now go!

—**Scott**

Aim High!

"It was the first entertainment that Walt Disney had ever designed expressly for children. 'But we're not going to talk down to the kids...Let's aim for the twelve-year-old. The younger ones will watch...they'll want to see what their older brothers and sisters are looking at.' "

—Bob Thomas on Walt Disney, *An American Original*

Walt Disney, the master of engaging children, knew that you have to aim high. In other words, if you're trying to connect with kids of various ages in a large-group setting, always target the oldest kids in the group. If you connect with the older kids, you'll grab the attention of all the kids.

Marketing experts know and practice this principle. We took their advice and created these guidelines for children's programming.

We target the oldest boy in the group. In other words, appeal to your oldest boys and you will appeal to everyone.

We choose music that will appeal to the oldest kids in the group. Know what style of music the oldest kids in your group are listening to. Nothing will turn off your group quicker than playing songs that sound too "babyish."

We feature older kids in our graphics and videos. Our elementary print pieces contain pictures of the oldest kids in the age group. If we do a video or skit involving kids, we normally use fifth- and sixth-graders as actors.

We use the oldest kids in the room on the praise team. If the oldest boys in your group are standing around with their hands in their pockets during worship, check who's leading. Our praise team is comprised of the oldest kids in the room, junior and senior high school students, plus adults.

We use clips from movies that upper elementary kids think are "cool." If your clips are from movies aimed at upper elementary kids, you'll engage all grades.

- Bring in upper elementary kids, and ask them to rate the "coolness" of your programming. They can quickly help you identify what needs to be adjusted.

- Take cues from preteen marketers. They can give you valuable ideas on how to connect with today's older kids.

—Dale

A Yellow Wall: Beating the Beige Blahs

Literally hundreds of churches have visited Dale's and my campuses. Dale's exciting "Fun Factory" and our crazy talking tree inspire and amaze. They're cool! "Of course they're cool," you're thinking. "If I had a million dollars to spend, I'd have a huge, cool ministry, too."

If you were to walk through my church today, you'd love the children's area. You'd love Dale's, too. Well, maybe you'd love them. They would affect you in one of two ways: either you'd be inspired…or you'd leave depressed.

Maybe your ministry will be blessed with the finances to do something big. Or maybe you'll never have a design budget. But you can do *something*. Here are some tips.

Make it up if you have to. I read an article once about this children's pastor in Arkansas, a guy with a vision. With little more than a willing team and a small ministry itching for something different, this guy literally changed the landscape of American children's ministry. The article laid out how his tiny team dreamed, researched, planned, and sweat like they were big. Partnering with a secular company (gasp!) whose portfolio included Universal Studios and Disney, they "innovented" a themed children's area. I had to meet this guy. I wrangled an introduction with Dale Hudson.

Dale graciously welcomed us. The instant he and I met, we connected. God had placed a similar dream in both our hearts. Dale let us kick his ministry's tires as he shared his story firsthand. We had our own ideas, stole many more from Dale, and returned abuzz, ready to create a space much better than we had originally envisioned.

Doing *something* may be hard, but doing *nothing* is well…nothing. Because of Dale's initial inspiration, today in large churches around the country you'll find slime machines, talking animals, two-story play structures, vibrant colors, amazing characters, and more. But if you had walked into either of our churches before our renovations, you would have left with the same impression: *They should do something!*

I heard Willie George once say, "I *refuse* to place children in a beige room, seat them at a table, make them fold their hands, listen quietly to my team tell them a story, and teach them that *this is God*. My God is a God of *color*. My God is the master artist of the universe. My God created leaves, grass, rainbows, our eyes, our skin. He's alive. All his creation is alive to praise him!" I nearly jumped out of my skin. Preach it, Willie! The picture you paint for the children of your ministry will influence how they view God. (Did you get that?) The environment you create will determine whether they want to come, and whether they'll bring friends.

Paint's cheap, and one person's trash is another's treasure. You don't need lots of money. Get stuff donated. Have people check their storage units, their garages, their closets. Dumpster dive. Get your hands on some cheap, colorful paint!

Our first kids' space was 100 percent commando volunteers working on a shoestring. We raided the storage barn and found some plastic-foam crosses that were used—once—in a cantata. We spray-painted them chrome and hung them from the ceiling. Volunteers built platforms from scraps, threw a paint party, found old light boards in a closet, and sewed fabric slip covers for the wall sound panels. Someone brought an old TV. Someone else donated a game system. When we were through, "The Zone" looked great!

More important, the kids loved it, and they loved being there. They brought their friends. And their friends loved it. And they all begged their parents to keep bringing them back. In the meantime, we taught them that God loved them, and we proved to them that *we* did. That was the start of who we are today, begun in drops of sweat and paint. One room at a time, LifeKIDS grew into the bright lights of today.

Little things grow. Luke 16:10 says, "If you are faithful in little things, you will be faithful in large ones."

Stop doing nothing; stop wishing. Do you somehow expect that will yield some magic opportunity later? That's not what Scripture says. Be faithful now. Work with the abilities and the resources you have, however little. God will entrust you with more.

Remember who this is for. Children love over-the-top! They love color. They love loud sounds and bright lights. If your children's area looks like a hotel conference room, or if it looks like your home, you missed it. Children are your target, not weekday businessmen. Make it fun. Make it loud. Make it cool!

See through the eyes of a child. I've repeatedly led my team on a crazy exercise. We crawled around our children's area on our knees. Have you ever done that? If you haven't, then you don't know what your kids' world looks like. Do it. Finish this paragraph, put this book down, and go for a walk… on your knees. Go (on your knees) to the restroom your kids are supposed to use. Try washing your hands that way. It's hard! Change your perspective. Most areas are designed for adults 5 feet tall and over.

Ask for help. Have a work day. Local businesses may happily donate products, if you can only muster the courage to ask. Invite art students from colleges and high schools. Ask your kids what's cool. Gather all the information you can, formulate your plan, and invite others to help.

To this day, people still reminisce about those crazy chrome crosses. Why? Those things have been gone for years. They remember…because they hung them!

Don't bite off more than you can chew. Be smart. Plan. Carve up what you need to do into phases. Execute just one phase at a time. Don't start a new room until the one you're working on is 100 percent complete—or you'll never finish.

Make it fun. Celebrate the changes as families arrive in their new spaces. Host your own version of *Extreme Makeover*. Invite. Involve. Engage.

Don't buy into all the easy excuses. You can paint a wall. You can build something. Anyone can. Even if it's for temporary or portable space. You can do *something*. Your kids will notice. Your ministry will change. Praise your Creator! Be creative, even as he is creative. Enjoy the color.

—Scott

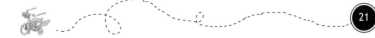

Today's kids are growing up in an experience-driven culture. They eat in restaurants such as The Rainforest Café and Chuck E. Cheese, where a meal is not just about food, it's about the whole themed experience. They experience rides at amusement parks that put them right in the middle of an unfolding, experiential story.

They play video games that let them experience new worlds and adventures. The computer has become a portal to unlimited experiences through virtual worlds, games, and online communities.

Let's be real. We can't compete. We'll never have the resources to match what kids experience on a daily basis outside of church. But we can still create service experiences where kids encounter God and his truth in memorable ways.

How? It's not as hard as you may think. Let's start from scratch.

Get a creative team together. It can be made up of anywhere from three to six people.

Decide what truth you are going to teach. Obviously the truth should come from a scriptural basis. Decide what key verse or Bible story you want to use.

Decide how you're going to "package" or "theme" the truth. The packaging or theme should be something culturally relevant to a child's world. We keep magazines such as Nickelodeon, Disney, and Kidscreen close by for ideas.

Begin tossing out ideas and writing them down. Even if an idea is not used, it will spark other ideas. Many times the craziest idea will be the seed that brings a great plan to fruition. Normally, when you hit gold everyone will know it. Everyone's eyes will light up when the idea is mentioned. It will just click.

Create your large-group experience. We use the large-group/small-group model. Here are the steps we follow to create a large-group experience.

- *Choose a worship song that reinforces the truth.* Worship is a key element in helping kids experience God's presence. The Bible tells us that God inhabits the praises of his people.

- *Use skits to reinforce the truth.* Use skits that involve real-life scenarios that kids face so they can see the truth lived out. Skits can be done live or by video.

- *Use games that illustrate the truth.* The first game should be high-energy, fun, and even messy. The second game can be more tame and can be a review tool.

- *Use a large-group lesson based on the truth or Bible story.* Make it fun and interactive. Use stories to illustrate the truth. (Personal stories from your own life are great.) Also be sure to use lots of visuals such as pictures and video clips.

Create your small-group experience. The kids have been sitting in large-group time. They have been participating, but maybe in a limited way. Small-group time makes the whole experience complete. Here are some tips for small-group time.

- *Make it interactive.* Kids want to talk. They want to be heard and known. So let them talk away. Use icebreaker questions and activities to get kids talking. Ask guided, open-ended questions that will get kids interacting.

- *Involve kids in the learning process.* Use crafts, activities, and games that get kids moving, participating, and having fun as they learn.

- *Include Scripture.* Go over the key Bible verse with kids. Use fun games and methods to help them remember it and understand its meaning.

- *Make it applicable.* Talk about real-life situations kids might face where they could apply what they've learned. Then create a specific challenge for the coming week where they can live out that truth.

- *Pray.* Let kids share prayer requests, and spend a few minutes praying with them for those needs. Rely on the Holy Spirit to move in kids' hearts so they can enjoy the greatest experience of all—God's presence.

—Dale

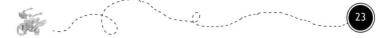

8

Are You Ready for a Miracle?

A huge crowd of people. A few loaves of bread. Even fewer fish.

And then a miracle where everyone's hunger was satisfied and their faith fed.

When things seem impossible, Jesus is ready to give you a miracle. As I've studied this passage over the years, I've always found great joy and peace in it. When it seemed like everything was out of control, God was ready to shine.

At times, we all face what seem to be impossible situations—there's just no money for this event; we don't have enough volunteers for the weekend; we've totally outgrown our facilities; we don't know which direction to go.

When we find ourselves on the brink of chaos, what lessons can we learn from this miracle of Jesus'?

Look out for the needs of others. Even with everything that was going on around him, who did Jesus care about? The crowd. He knew they were hungry and needed to be fed. Always be aware of the needs of your team, your volunteers, and the families of your ministry.

Remember who's sitting on the hill with you. The disciples had been with Jesus. They knew his power. They had seen the miracles. And yet they thought, "There's no way we can do this." No matter what you're facing, you're not alone. You have Jesus. He's with you, and he can do more than you can ask, think, or imagine.

Look for something he can work with. Andrew, Peter's brother, said, "There's a young boy here…" God always provides a way. Many times it won't make sense to you. But be on the lookout for something God can work with in your situation.

Believe. Even after bringing a potential solution to Christ, Andrew followed up with, "But what good is that with this huge crowd?" When you come to God, come with faith. No buts, just faith.

Get ready for your miracle. God's ready, he's able, and he loves to demonstrate his mighty power. As we face difficult, even impossible, situations, he will show himself strong and provide us with more than we ever imagined.

Sometimes it may seem as though the odds are stacked against you. In those times, God wants to come through for you! He's waiting to blow your mind. So look around, ask him for faith to believe, and get ready!

—**Scott**

9

Mirror, Mirror, on the Wall, Who's the Leader of Them All?

Your ministry is a direct reflection of your leadership. If you've been in your current position for more than two years, it's a mirror of your leadership. Take a look in the mirror of your ministry. Then ask yourself these questions.

Am I contributing or conforming? Great leaders don't just conform to the way things are. They contribute ideas, strategy, and vision. They bring a lot to the table instead of just going along with the way things have always been done. Look at your ministry. Is it contributing or conforming? Either way, it's coming from you.

Am I passionate or passive? Do you have passion for your ministry? Is it a fire that burns in your heart? Can people hear the excitement in your voice as you talk about what God is doing? Or are you just going through the motions? Have you lost that first love? Are you just getting a paycheck or fulfilling a necessary task? If the people in your ministry are passionate, it's coming from you. If they're passive, it's coming from you.

Am I motivating or maintaining? Are you motivating your team to do great things for God? Are you helping them take steps to grow as leaders? Are you getting them pumped up to go to the next level? Or is your team in maintenance mode? Just hanging in there, trying to keep the boat afloat, turned inward to maintain what you've got instead of reaching out to those outside your four walls? The difference between the ministry being motivated or just maintaining is you.

Am I dreaming or drifting? Do you have your eye on the future? Are you asking God to infuse you with a vision so big that it would be impossible to do it without him? Great leaders dream big dreams. They don't just drift along aimlessly with no thought of the future. Is your ministry reflecting big dreams?

Do you want to improve the reflection you see in the mirror? I know I do. To be honest, I'm not always happy with what I see. I'm sure you feel the same way at times. Here are some ways to make your leadership reflection look better.

Renew. Renew. Renew. Ever forget to recharge your cell phone? The next morning you know the battery is low, but you decide to go ahead and try to use it anyway. Later, at the worst time possible, the battery goes out on you. It reminds you that if you're going to use the cell phone, you've got to keep it charged up. Your spiritual life is the same way. Ministry and leadership will quickly empty your tank. If you don't refill yourself spiritually, your team will soon begin to notice a glazed look in your eyes. Stay connected to Jesus. Spend time with him through God's Word and prayer.

Read. Read. Read. Read a variety of books, magazines, websites, and blogs. Read about leadership, children's ministry, technology, cultural issues and shifts, business ideas and practices, marketing, and more. What you read will directly affect what you see staring back at you in the ministry mirror.

Evaluate. Evaluate. Evaluate. Don't just see what you want to see in the mirror. Take an honest look at your leadership. What are your strengths? What are your weaknesses? Gather some people around you who will help you evaluate your leadership.

Change. Change. Change. You must be willing to change if you're going to stay relevant. Just because you were connected to the culture a year ago doesn't mean you are today. Hold ministry methods loosely in your hands. The leader you are today is not the leader that your team will need in two years. Be willing to change.

Network. Network. Network. Go to relevant conferences. Meet other children's ministry leaders in your area for lunch. Talk regularly with other leaders by phone. Stay connected.

Network with young leaders who have been in children's ministry for a short time. Learn from their passion, fresh ideas, and relevant thinking. Network with people who have been in ministry for about the same amount of time as you. They face many of the same challenges you face. They are doing things that you can learn from. You can encourage each other as you journey together. Network with leaders who have been in ministry a lot longer than you. Learn from their wisdom, mistakes, and successes.

Mirror, mirror, on the wall, who's the leader of them all? The answer is—you! May your ministry mirror become a reflection of all that God wants to accomplish in and through your life.

—**Dale**

Do More by Doing Less

Do you ever feel like there are just not enough hours in the day? Do you ever feel like you just can't get it all done? Stop trying. Seriously! As your ministry grows…as your responsibility grows…the only real way to do more is to do less.

Build something that will scale. (Preferably up.) Let me give you an example. Our ministry has been multi-site for years now. We went from one campus to two, from two to three, and eventually to our current total of 12! (And more are on the way.) In fact, our pastor's vision is 50 total campuses! To achieve growth like this, we had to have a plan for campus team growth. We used several indicators—number of kids, number of volunteers, number of services. Here's what our progression plan ultimately looked like:

Phase 1: Director
Phase 2: Director/Ministry Coordinator
Phase 3: Director/Ministry Coordinator/Cast Member Relations
Phase 4: Director/Ministry Coordinator/Cast Member Relations/
Experience Coordinator
Phase 5: Director/Ministry Coordinator/Cast Member Relations/
Experience Coordinator/Administrative Assistant

Be all things to all people (at first)…This model carried each campus through every stage of its natural growth, from a brand-new campus with 50 kids to a 10-year-old campus with 2,500. It's a great model. But look again at that first phase. Did you notice that there's only one position? Director. Job description: everything. Literally. That position is responsible for everything, and the first hire has to do it all! It's not until the next phase when we add another staff member. Even then, the director is still responsible for everything, but he or she is no longer *doing* everything. This kind of progression continues through all the phases.

...then lead. While the director's responsibility grows with the ministry, the actual hands-on responsibilities decrease. Instead, these tasks are delegated to trusted team members and faithful volunteers. The leader's role evolves into its simplest definition: "one who leads." That person becomes the voice of the ministry, the vision-caster for the staff. This person is the voice of reason in times of conflict, the voice of experience in times of uncertainty, and the voice of calm during a storm.

A simple plan: Do more and more, and less and less. Does that make sense? It's not about you. (If you think it is, you need to get over yourself.) Once you realize that, you empower the others around you, you further the vision, and you more efficiently fulfill the call God has placed on your life. So how do you start?

- *Realize what only you can do.* Specifically, write down the five areas of your greatest gifting. Commit to do *just those things* for your ministry.

- *Focus on your strengths.* Do what you do best. Hire team members and line up volunteers for everything else the ministry needs. Allow them to shine where they're gifted, which will strengthen your team and build community.

- *Never rely on payroll.* God has placed willing and able people around all of us who want to be a part of our ministry. Ask God to open your eyes to see those people in your sphere of influence, and then boldly ask them to volunteer their time to further the kingdom.

- *Allow your team to shine.* People—especially leaders—are often willing to push themselves beyond what they thought they were capable of. These same people often will not allow their team members to experience that same sense of accomplishment, artificially limiting their responsibilities. Why? Fear of failure? Fear of competition? These are questions you should ask yourself. Push your team. Allow them to discover their real potential.

Find the help you need, stop playing the martyr, and watch your ministry grow beyond what you ever thought it could.

Do more by doing less!

—Scott

11

Go With the Flow!

I have a confession to make. It's extremely hard for me to take off my children's pastor glasses when I'm being entertained.

At the movies, I'm thinking about how they're using the background music, camera angles, and special effects to engage the audience. When I'm on an interactive ride at Disney World, instead of enjoying the ride, I'm hanging out of the car to see where the projector is placed, how the animatronics are laid out, and thinking through how they are capturing the attention of the kids around me. When I'm watching TV or a DVD at home, I'm thinking of how I can use a video clip from it to illustrate a lesson or motivate our leaders.

It's all part of being a children's pastor...I guess.

I love to watch the inner workings of entertainment that engages, captivates, and motivates people. I love to see the dreaming, planning, scenes, props, videos, lighting, and sound all come together to give people an experience they will never forget. I think about the hundreds or even thousands of hours of hard work that went into making it happen.

I also love to watch kids being engaged, excited, inspired, and encouraged through a carefully planned experience at church. It's awesome to see their smiles when they hear that God loves them, to hear their giggles and laughter when they experience something funny, and to see the sincerity in their faces as they pray and worship.

It takes strategic planning bathed in prayer to make this happen. After years of watching, learning, and fine-tuning, we have come up with the following service flow. We have found that kids respond extremely well to these elements.

This flow is based on a large-group/small-group format, with the actual lesson lasting about one hour. It can be adjusted to fit different time schedules.

Service Flow for Elementary Kids

Pre-Service Activities (15 minutes)

- Leaders hang out with kids, play video games, watch a music video on screen, play board games, and utilize craft tables.

Service Countdown (5 minutes)

- Kids gather to large-group area during this time. The video countdown is shown on screen.
- Have high-energy leaders on stage during this time to help kids interact with the video. Mix it up and instead of using a video countdown each week, sometimes have leaders lead kids in cheers, tell jokes, toss beach balls, and so on.

Welcome (1 minute)

- A high-energy leader welcomes kids to the service, goes over rules, leads a cheer, and gets kids on their feet for the first worship song.

Song (4 minutes)

- This song should be very high-energy. It's important that the first song be a fast song.

Opening Host/Co-Host (3 minutes)

- This is a two-person team that introduces the lesson for the day and has the kids repeat the point, or core teaching truth. This segment is done live or on video, depending on the series.

- The host is a normal, level-headed character who is introducing the truth/lesson from a serious perspective. The co-host is a cutup, prankster-type character who acts as though he or she knows all about the teaching truth but doesn't have a clue about what it means.
- The co-host has a conflict, issue, or life situation related to the teaching truth that must be resolved. It is set up during this time.

Game Time (4 minutes)

- Use a high-energy, Nickelodeon-style game that involves two teams of kids. Think fast-paced and messy. The game is tied to the teaching truth.

Song and Offering (3 minutes)

- This song should be slower and bring the energy level down.
- Have offering buckets up front, and tell the kids they can bring up their offerings during the song. Pray for the offering before you start the song.

Skit (3 minutes)

- Try a skit that involves real-life scenarios that relate directly to the lesson.

Lesson (10 minutes)

- A good communicator teaches the lesson. He or she uses a

variety of methods including video, audience interaction, object lessons, and props.

- Close the lesson with prayer.
- Transition to small groups.

Small Groups (22 minutes)

- Group six to eight kids with a leader.
- Use the following elements:
    Plug In (share about their week)
    Charge Up (go over Bible verse)
    Live Out (hands-on activity with life application)
    Pass It On (talk about who they can invite to church)
    Closing prayer (take requests and pray)

Transition Back to Large Group (1 minute)

Closing Host/Co-Host (2 minutes)

- The co-host now understands the core teaching truth and his or her conflict has been resolved. The host patiently endures the co-host's antics.
- The host or co-host repeats the core teaching truth with kids again.

Review Game (4 minutes)

- A high-energy game show where kids review the lesson and those from previous weeks.
- Review game is played until parents start coming.

Dismissal

- Praise team leads kids in a high-energy song or two as parents walk through to pick them up. This allows parents to see their kids worshipping and to feel the energy and excitement of the room. Many times parents will stop and begin worshipping with their kids.

—**Dale**

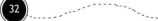

12

Don't Feed the Bears...
Feed the Leaders

We are called to lead children, to point them toward a relationship with a loving, living Savior. There's no greater privilege, no greater call. To carry it out, we're privileged to work with adult volunteers.

I've always embraced who I am, what my ministry is. I was called to minister to children. Sure, I *can* visit effectively with adults, but that's not my greatest strength. But even though it's not my strong suit, I have learned to love leading adult volunteers. You can, too. Here's how:

Maintain frequent two-way communication. If you can personally call each one of your volunteers once a month, do it. If that's unrealistic, learn how to send customized e-mail messages.

Be forewarned: Messing this up is potentially worse than doing nothing at all. Nothing feels worse than getting what you think is a personal e-mail or note from a leader, only to realize later that you and 5,000 of your children's pastor's "dearest friends" are all listed in the "To" box.

If you send e-mails, place the basic text you want to use in one location, and then copy and paste it into a message. Then—and this is the important part—personalize it. Using the volunteer's name (or even better, a nickname). Mention something you know about the person.

Never stop training. Every ministry, regardless of size, should have no fewer than two training events per year. When you can, divide the events according to areas of service or age groups. Don't make it easy and convenient for you—make it easy and convenient for your volunteers.

Make training fun! In our elementary area, we don't call them training sessions. We call them dance parties. Volunteers come to learn the motions to new and existing songs that we use, and we take that opportunity to share anything else we need to. They love it.

Value their time. Be prepared! Make sure that when they leave, there's no question it was worth it to them to give up an evening or afternoon.

Prove your love. Hold social appreciation events at least once a year with the sole intention of honoring your volunteers. Love them. Play games, have fun, eat, and get to know each other as real human beings, not roles. This isn't rocket science: Training events are for training, and appreciation events are for appreciation.

Cast your vision. At least once a year, gather your volunteers to celebrate what God has done in the past year and cast vision for the next year. This is a vital component of keeping people engaged. They'll lose passion over time and forget why they're doing it…unless you remind them.

Maintain as much personal contact as possible. Nothing says "Hey, you don't matter much to me" like seeing your children's pastor fly by in the hall, not even acknowledging your presence. Stop. Say hello. People are more important than programs. Tell your volunteers how glad you are that they're there.

Pray. The two best ways you can minister to your volunteers are to pray for them and equip them to pray for each other. One of my star team members, Julie, created a weekly e-mail chain where our volunteers can add prayer requests and praise reports. We send it—individually, of course—to every volunteer who wants to receive it. The results have been amazing. People ask each other about these issues on the weekend, and it has really drawn the team together with true concern.

One last thing. If the tasks on your list or your number of programs make it too difficult for you to nurture your volunteers and build relationships, *then cut the tasks and reduce the programs.* Don't let the "good things" suffocate the "best things." God loves people more than he loves programs.

Never forget: This is all about the people.

—**Scott**

The "Eyes" Have It!

If you want to effectively communicate to today's kids, then you'd better go visual. Leonard Sweet, one of my favorite authors and a forward church thinker, reminds us of the importance of communicating visually. He says, "Research shows the brain's ability to read print on a page is about 100 bits per second. The brain's ability to take in images is about a billion bits per second. You do the math." Here are some ways to go visual so you can "see" great results.

Make an icon for each key truth you teach. Over time, kids will remember the key truths when they see the icons. For example, if one of your truths is "God wants me to take a step in my spiritual growth," then perhaps your icon could be a footprint. After kids see the footprint icon a few times, they will begin linking it to the truth.

Show Bible stories instead of telling them. There are great videos for almost every story in the Bible. Many videos show Bible stories quoted word for word from Scripture. There is so much power in communicating Bible stories visually.

Use visual objects and images when teaching. When you teach, illustrate what you are saying. For example, if you are teaching about Satan tempting Eve in the Garden of Eden, have a rubber snake and an apple in your hand. If you are talking about a lion, show a picture of a lion.

> There are some great books to help you locate movie clips for teaching. Check out *Movie Clips for Kids*, *Movie Clips for Kids—The Sequel*, and *Blockbuster Movie Illustrations* by Group.

Use video clips to illustrate your lessons. One of the most effective ways to visually connect with today's kids is to show video clips that illustrate what you're teaching. Here's an example. You're talking about faith. You could pause and say, "Check this out." On screen comes the scene of Indiana Jones standing and looking across a large ravine. Suddenly he closes his eyes and steps forward onto an invisible stone bridge he was told would catch him. What a great picture of faith! Kids love it!

Obviously, you need to use wisdom and discretion when showing clips. Make sure they are age-appropriate. Depending on your church culture, you might even want to inform parents ahead of time about the clip you will be showing. Also, make sure your church has a licensing agreement that allows you to show short clips for no profit.

Make your own videos. Grab a camera, and make a video. How about doing your lesson on video occasionally? How about making your announcements by video? How about a skit on video? How about video interviews on important topics? Get the kids involved. Let them help produce and be in the videos. Most computers have simple editing software. You can do it. If you have the time, budget, and resources, make it higher quality. But hey, this is the day of YouTube. High quality or low quality…videos are effective.

Mix it up. Kids need a variety of visual communication. Some weeks make the entire lesson on video. Some weeks teach live and use visual props. Some weeks use pictures on the screen as you teach. Some weeks use movie clips. Mix it up. Even visual communication can become a rut if you don't change it up.

Jesus emphasized the importance of the eye in Matthew 6:22–23. The eye is a direct link to inside a person. It has been called the window of the soul.

As we speak the communication language of this visual generation, we will gain access to their hearts.

—**Dale**

Don't Raise Your Hand

I love to teach live. The bigger the crowd, the better. I love seeing the faces of kids as they engage and participate in the message, game, or song. While your ministry may look different from ours, the following principles will transcend denomination and style and will touch the hearts of the kids you're ministering to.

Why would you want to duplicate school? In our ministry, we do everything we can to stay away from resembling school. Why? Kids spend a pretty big chunk of their waking hours sitting in a school classroom. Plus, most kids don't love school. Even those who do are happy to get out every once in awhile.

See through a child's eyes. In this generation, we must grab kids' attention to engage them. Go spend one day in a typical elementary school. You'll see mountains of worksheets, comprehension questions, hand raising, sitting still, and lots of reading, writing, and homework.

Now think like a kid. What compels you to engage? What makes you want to be there? As you ask God to reveal his will for your ministry, ask him to help you think like a child. Ask for insight into the world of contemporary children.

Bring in outside consultation. So many companies today specialize in décor, curriculum, and activities to engage children. Ask them what's working in other places. Allow them to offer you new options and alternatives.

Bring in a focus group of kids. Kids are remarkably creative, they're full of great new ideas, and they love for grown-ups to ask for their opinions.

Go on a field trip. Visit places that are engaging to children. I can't go anywhere anymore and not be "working." From the mall to Chuck E. Cheese to Disneyland, I'm constantly looking at what materials they're using for their signage, what color palettes they're using, and how they separate areas for specific age groups. I also look at which characters have stood the test of time and which new ones seem to be working. The world around you is full of success stories of how to relate to kids. Learn from them!

We must engage our kids. We must find ways to create environments and experiences that will make them want to return, and make them want to bring their friends. We do everything we can to stay far, far away from anything that looks remotely like school. It means we jump up and down during the game. It means we have fun with hand motions during worship. It means we laugh out loud. It means that when I ask you a question, I want you to scream out your answer...

But don't you dare raise your hand!

—**Scott**

Vision...the Leadership Tool You Must Have in Your Ministry Tool Belt!

> "The very essence of leadership is that you have to have a vision."
>
> —Theodore Hesburgh, American clergyman
> and university president

As a children's minister, you need a lot of leadership tools in your ministry tool belt: wisdom, perseverance, team-building, creativity, faithfulness, enthusiasm.

But if you asked me to choose the most important leadership tool a children's minister needs (thanks for asking, by the way), I would quickly say... *vision.*

Vision will decide if you settle for mediocrity or move forward with urgency. Vision will shape your future. Vision will take the ministry you lead to heights no one ever dreamed possible.

Vision brings growth. Has your ministry reached its plateau? Have you gotten accustomed to lack of growth? Vision will not allow you to stay there. Vision will look at kids and families outside your church walls and find ways to reach them. Vision will passionately pursue those without Christ.

Our children's ministry has experienced tremendous growth in the past few years. Our rooms are packed. It would be easy to sit back and rest in what God has done. But vision won't allow us to do that. Our eyes must be turned upon the fields that are ripe for harvest. There are thousands of kids and families all around us that we have not yet reached. We must pray, plan, make room, and keep pursuing the vision to reach people for Christ in our city.

Vision brings leaders. Vision is your number-one recruiting tool! People want to be a part of a God-sized vision. People will follow vision. Instead of trying to recruit out of need...recruit with vision! Share with people the vision God has placed in your heart, and watch people start getting on board.

Our executive pastor, Mike Bodine, recently came to our Family Ministries staff meeting and shared the vision of reaching our city for Christ. He talked about staying awake at night with tears running down his face as he prayed for the people in our city who need Christ. He laid out strategic plans that will help us reach them. As he shared the vision, my heart began to burn inside me. I was reminded of why God called me to Las Vegas. It's a vision I can give my life to. When you share a vision that is from God…people will follow it!

Vision brings life. A children's ministry that is full of life and energy is being infused with vision. A children's ministry that is on life-support is fading away because there is a lack of vision. The vitality level of your children's ministry is directly linked to your vision level.

Vision brings finances. Need more money for your ministry? Vision can bring it. People will financially back a God-given vision.

In 1999, the children's ministry I had been called to lead was meeting in a chapel. The chapel had beige walls, stained-glass windows, and was used for funerals during the week. Any room where you can comfortably hold funerals is not a good room for children's ministry!

I began to seek God, and he placed a vision in my heart for a new children's area that would be a kid magnet. I shared the vision with my pastor, Dr. Ronnie Floyd, and he also believed the vision was from God. He set up a meeting for me to take the vision to the finance committee. I'll never forget preparing that presentation and then walking into the boardroom. The vision would cost a lot of money to become a reality. I silently wondered if the board would be willing to commit. The chairman of the board had to leave a few minutes early that night. As I ended my presentation, he stood and said, "I believe in this. I think we should do it." At that moment, I knew God was sending the finances to make the vision a reality.

That vision became the fully animated children's worship area called Toon Town. It became a catalyst that inspired churches across America to build kid-friendly environments. Finances follow vision.

Vision changes lives. Lives are changed when someone fulfills God's vision for his or her life. God gave one man I know a vision to plant a church in North Las Vegas. He followed his vision, and the church was launched. Hundreds of people have already been reached. Vision that is born and fueled by God will change lives.

Do you have a vision for your ministry? The kind of vision that keeps you awake at night? The kind of vision that you are willing to give your life to?

The kind of vision that you can't help but talk about? The kind of vision that you eat, breathe, and sleep?

If you do, then keep pursuing that vision. Keep believing God for it. Don't let anything stop you from seeing it become a reality. If the vision has grown dim in your heart, ask God to rekindle it afresh and anew. If you don't have a vision for your ministry yet, start seeking God for it. He has the vision waiting for your leadership tool belt. Ask him for it, and he'll place it there for you. When that happens, nothing will ever be the same again!

—**Dale**

16

Don't Worry, Be Happy

Remember that song? I love that melody: "Don't worry…Be happy…" How are you doing with that? Seriously, where your ministry is concerned, how's the worry thing going for you?

Worry often comes when we've taken control rather than relying on God to meet our needs and make our way. We may worry when we haven't adequately prepared and we're unsure where we stand. We may worry when we overextend. But worry doesn't come from God! Paul wrote to the church at Philippi:

"Don't worry about anything; instead, pray about everything. Tell God what you need, and thank him for all he has done. Then you will experience God's peace, which exceeds anything we can understand. His peace will guard your hearts and minds as you live in Christ Jesus" (Philippians 4:6-7).

I love this New Living Translation version of this passage. I've taught it to kids several times over the years. It's like a recipe, a plan for success. If you do this, this will be the result. Simple, huh? It should be. Let's break down this verse:

Don't worry. Stop right there! Don't worry. That's about as clear as it gets, isn't it? Don't worry.

About anything. *But Lord! You don't know these volunteers. But Lord, I don't know how to do this. I don't know where to start!*

No, those count as "things." He says, "Don't worry about anything."

Instead…Not along with. Not as a last resort. Not when you've done everything you can do on your own. *Instead* means "to take the place of." Instead of worrying—do this…

Pray. Take advantage of the opportunity you have to talk to the Father of the universe, your creator, the one true God. Speak to him, and listen to him. His network never misses a call. Just pray.

About everything. Not just the big things. Not just the little things. *Everything!*

Tell God what you need. Your loving Father—who loves to pour out good gifts to his children—is listening. Your Father—who has plans to prosper you—is waiting for you to ask. He's waiting for you to acknowledge that you have a need. He already knows…

Thank him for all he's done. Praise him. Is the situation you're in bigger than one he's carried you through before? Give him praise. He is able. He is worthy. He's done it before. Be encouraged. He'll do it again!

Then you will experience God's peace. *But Lord, you don't understand what I'm going through!* Take heart—he does understand. God *is* peace.

It's a recipe. A game plan. A promise from the King of all kings, the Lord of all lords. So why are you worried? God's on the throne. He's faithful.

Don't worry, be happy.

—**Scott**

17

The Blank Piece of Paper!

"Therefore, go and make disciples of all the nations, baptizing them in the name of the Father and the Son and the Holy Spirit. Teach these new disciples to obey all the commands I have given you. And be sure of this: I am with you always, even to the end of the age."

—Matthew 28:19-20

In this passage, Jesus gave us our marching orders. Simply put...we are here to reach people who are far from God and help them become followers of Christ.

Would you like to measure the effectiveness of your ministry based on Jesus' command? Here's how to do it:

Grab a blank piece of paper and a pen. At the top, write the program or event that you want to evaluate. Here's the next step. If it's an event, write "How many children and families were reached or took a spiritual step because of this event?" If it's an ongoing program, write this: "How many children and families are being reached or taking spiritual steps because of this program?"

Now here's the big test. Can you write down names? Real names of real people who were reached or took spiritual steps? If you're struggling to write names, then it's time to take a hard look at the program or event.

We can do lots of things in ministry. We can fill our church calendar with events, programs, choirs, trips, and much more. But the bottom line is, whatever we are doing must effectively reach people and help them take spiritual steps if we are going to obey Jesus.

Are you willing to put your ministry programs to this test? Are you willing to put your events to this test? Are you willing to put tradition to this test? If so, are you then willing to make changes based on the results?

Here's an example. You put on a festival. You and your team spend hundreds and hundreds of hours in preparation. You also spend a sizable amount of your budget on it. You have a great turnout. It's now eight months later, and you're getting ready to prepare for next year's festival. Before you do, stop and put the festival to the test. Get out the blank piece of paper and see if you can write down any names. Are there any new families who were reached and are now regular attendees of your church? If you can't write down any names, then consider the validity of the event. Yeah, I know...everyone had a great time and you had tons of people there...it was a safe place for the kids to get candy...but, where are the names? Could all the time, energy, and resources be poured into a more effective event or program?

I know what some are thinking...you can't always see the results...even if only one person comes to Christ it's worth it...but we've been doing that program for years...I became a Christ-follower years ago because of that event...our church members will be offended if we drop that event...on and on we could go.

The bottom line is Matthew 28:19-20. Nothing else matters. Not our traditions, not our programs...not our big events. If those things are effectively fulfilling Matthew 28:19-20, then great! But if not, then how long are you going to stare at that blank piece of paper?

Jesus doesn't want that paper to be blank. He wants to fill it with names of kids, moms, and dads in your city! So take the test...face the results...and do what you need to do to fill it up with names!

—**Dale**

18

Faith Like That

Who inspires you? Who's doing what you want to do? Whose heart has the Holy Spirit connected you with? Who do you want to be when you grow up?

Get down with what God's up to. God let my pastor and me in on his vision for multiple campuses, blessing us with the burden to depart from live teaching to pre-produced video. I had been teaching live eight times every weekend for more than a year, shuttling back and forth between two campuses seven miles apart. Then leadership announced we were rolling out number 3. Our newest campus was an hour and a half's drive away! Nobody mentioned a helicopter, so something had to change. My pastor was already experimenting with video, so we followed his lead, pre-producing our elementary curriculum on DVD, which was pretty novel at the time.

Seek out kindred spirits, and bond with them. At about the same time, I was wandering through a children's ministry convention in Dallas, and I stumbled upon an amazing booth with plasma TVs, loud music, cool graphics, and a short guy in a costume. It was KIDMO's first conference. As I stood gawking at their terrific content, Johnny Rogers, KIDMO's lead teacher, and I immediately bonded. They were doing what we were doing, only *a lot* better! Johnny introduced me to the gang. We excitedly explained our vision and our needs, and discussed how we thought they could help us achieve our objectives. The rest is history. Much more than just a resource, I found a mentor (and a friend). This goofy man has taught me exponentially about grabbing the hearts of children. Their company has survived growth pains, just as we have. They've taken big risks in trying new things, just as we have. And I'm a better minister today because of their example.

Imitate greatness where you find it. In 1 Corinthians 4:16, Paul said, "So I urge you to imitate me." I love this verse. Paul, with no hint of pride but with a confidence that just blows my mind, writes to the church of Corinth: "Hey! Do what I do!" Go Paul. Go God.

If you're reading this book, there's a great chance you're located somewhere in America, a nation blessed with amazing Christian leaders and resources. We're surrounded by churches, pastors, children's directors, and worship leaders who are literally "the best of the best." And yet, so many churches try to create a round thingy to transport their ministry from point A to point B. News flash: It's called *the wheel*...and it already exists. Watch what great leaders are doing. Then you try to do it, too.

Mod your ride. Hear me clearly. I'm *not* saying that you should blindly mimic what everyone else is doing. God placed a unique vision inside you. Pursue it. Don't plan or model your ministry completely after something else. What I *am* saying is that, in areas where you haven't come into your own yet, imitate others. Do you really need to create your ministry's requisition forms from scratch? Probably not. Examine what has worked for others, and try that. Identify what things blew up, and don't try those!

Maybe your ideal mentor is a well-known children's minister. Maybe it's the person who previously held your position. Maybe it's the faithful volunteer who's served in children's ministry longer than you've been a believer. Whoever it is, wherever they are, find them. Listen. Watch. Learn. Read their books. Follow their blogs. Pray for them. God placed them in your life and in your ministry for a reason, and for a season. Take full advantage of that blessing.

—**Scott**

> "But you will receive power when the Holy Spirit comes upon you. And you will be my witnesses, telling people about me everywhere—in Jerusalem, throughout Judea, in Samaria, and to the ends of the earth."

—Acts 1:8

We are called to reach people everywhere. And it all starts in our own city, in our own Jerusalem. If we're going to be effective, we must know our local culture.

Missionaries to other countries go to great lengths to learn and adapt to the foreign culture. They immerse themselves in the language, customs, practices, food, and many times even the dress, of that culture. They realize they must connect with the people if they are going to have the opportunity to share the good news with them.

We must each become a student of our local culture if we're going to reach those around us. Here are some questions to ask yourself as you seek to know your Jerusalem better.

Where is my Jerusalem located? A rural culture will be different from an urban culture. A northern culture will be different from a southern one. I have served in churches in several different areas of the country. Each area was unique, and I had to adapt each time. Be willing to adjust as needed to connect with the people in your Jerusalem.

I moved to Las Vegas from a church in the south. All the kids there called me "Brother Dale." But not in Vegas...if you call someone "brother," you'll get funny looks. I'm just "Dale" here, and I like it. I'm not about to ask kids to call me "Brother Dale." It's not a fit in my current Jerusalem.

IDEA

- If you grew up in the area where you serve, you have a huge advantage in knowing the culture. If you didn't, then ask questions, observe, and become a student of the people.

What are the demographics of my Jerusalem? Demographic studies for your Jerusalem are just an online click away. Find out the ages, family structures, and median incomes of the people. Then use that information to help you target families. For example, is your area made up of many young families? How can you reach out to them? Is it made up of lots of senior adults? Many of them may be helping raise their grandkids. Could you reach out to these grandparents with a support group?

What are families' schedules like in my Jerusalem? Is your Jerusalem a slower-paced culture? Is your Jerusalem full of soccer leagues, baseball teams, hunting seasons, trips to the lake? Know the pace of family life in your culture. Know what families spend their time doing.

Then plan your service schedule accordingly. Be willing to adjust programs and ministries that are not in line with people's schedules. The struggling program you are trying to keep propped up may not be dying due to lack of quality. It may be because only a handful of people can get there at that time.

What is the weather like in my Jerusalem? In our area, summer is our winter. What I mean is this…people stay indoors during the summer months due to the extreme heat. Kids aren't outside playing on summer days. You can't do outdoor activities or outings many times due to the heat.

The weather in your Jerusalem will affect your attendance, programming, and activities. Use wisdom in planning based on your local weather patterns. This will help you maximize your outreach to the community.

What is the school schedule in my Jerusalem? Obtain a list of the local school schedules. Use it as a tool in planning. Again, use wisdom and work with school schedules and not against them to maximize planning.

Also, follow your schools' age grouping to determine when kids move from elementary to junior high ministry. If sixth-graders are part of junior high in your area, they may not be happy about still being in the children's ministry at church that year.

What are the needs of my Jerusalem? At first glance, our city is glamorous. It's called the entertainment capital of the world. Some of the most elaborate hotels, resorts, and buildings in the world can be found here. Stars and celebrities are always in town. It's paradise for people who love to party and live the fast life.

But behind the glitz and glamour are people with desperate needs. Our city is known as the wedding capital of the world with more than 110,000 weddings performed each year, but it also has one of the highest divorce rates in the world. Behind all the partying, smiles, and laughter is one of the highest suicide rates in the country. We see people who have lost everything because of gambling addictions. Families are being torn apart by drug use.

Everything in Vegas is extreme. The hotels are extreme. The gambling is extreme. The lust is extreme. The food buffets are extreme. The entertainment is extreme. The heat is extreme. Many people live hard. You can see it in their faces. They are desperately searching for something…trying to find fulfillment…trying to find happiness. And the cool thing is we have the privilege of sharing with them the answer to all their needs.

Recently, my wife was leading a small group of second-grade girls. One little girl said she wants to be a stripper when she grows up. Unfortunately, that's part of the culture she lives in. But we saw the privilege to share God's plan with her.

Do you know the culture of your area? Do you have your finger on the pulse of the people in your city? Do you know what issues and problems they are facing?

How can I effectively reach out to my Jerusalem? In our Jerusalem, we have found that people respond to grace. Las Vegas is known as "Sin City" to the rest of the world, but to us it is known as "Grace City." In fact, in each of our offices is a picture of the strip that says above it "Grace City." Many people walk through our doors in desperate need of grace. They have lived life hard and have hit bottom. They need to know there is hope…there is forgiveness…there is grace through Jesus.

Each Jerusalem is unique. You have to discover the needs of the kids and families in your area and then determine the most effective way to reach out to them. God has called you to your own Jerusalem…not someone else's. Many times we go to conferences and see something that is working in another part of the country. We come back and try to implement it only to see it flop. There is no substitute for knowing your Jerusalem and fulfilling the unique plan God has for your ministry.

Know your Jerusalem…engage its culture…and watch God use your ministry to see lives changed!

—**Dale**

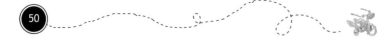

Here I Am to Worship

Can you believe how great the songs are in children's ministry today? They're cool! They're even actually cool enough that kids will hear them on the radio and get them stuck in their heads. I know I do!

As great as it is, when I consider music in our ministry, I still long for something more. Don't get me wrong...I love seeing hundreds of kids rocking out and moving in unison to a song. But nothing touches my heart, nothing gets me more jazzed, than seeing a child *really* worshipping Jesus.

When worshipping, don't forget to truly worship. I pray that we never forget that there's a time for all kinds of worship—some loud and crazy, but also some soft and some reverent. It's never been our desire only to entertain kids. While that is absolutely *one* of our objectives, I want to teach our children that worship is an honor, that it's truly an invitation from our Creator to enter his holy of holies and fall down on our faces before him. We should give him praise for the mighty things he's done and for who he is, was, and will forever be.

Worship is a powerful medium. For many, God speaks as much through the music as he does through the spoken Word. We have the great responsibility to lead children in worship—not in songs—but in worship. Here are a few tips to use with your worship leaders.

Kids don't care about your voice. So many people are afraid to lead worship because they think their voices aren't good enough. Kids don't care. As the psalmist wrote, make a joyful "noise."

Get involved... Model reverent worship for kids during the slower songs, and have fun with the faster ones. Kids love to see adults genuinely engaged.

...just not *too* involved. I once had a leader who would get so into the songs that he would totally zone out, forgetting about the kids. We always want to model worship, but we have to remember why we're there—to lead.

(By the way, when you're in a room full of kids, it's always a good idea to keep one eye open!)

Worship. Lead the room, keep control, and have fun. But don't miss the opportunity to genuinely worship your King.

—**Scott**

21

Adios Amigo!

"At this point many of his disciples turned away and deserted him. Then Jesus turned to the Twelve and asked, 'Are you also going to leave?'"

—John 6:66-67

It's inevitable. It happened to Jesus, and it will happen to you in ministry. People will walk away. Volunteers that you have poured your life into will decide they no longer want to be a part of the team. Families that you have helped and invested major time in will decide they are going to attend another church. Kids that you love will be pulled away by parents who no longer agree with the direction of the church.

What do you do when people leave?

Acknowledge the pain. When someone leaves, acknowledge the pain. It's OK to be sad. It's OK to hurt. It's OK to shed some tears. Your pain is actually a great sign. It shows that you truly care for people and are investing your life in them.

Take your pain to Jesus. He has felt what you are feeling. Spend time talking to him about it. Release your pain to him. He will be your greatest encourager.

Don't take it personally. When I first started in ministry, I thought it was my fault when people left. I thought I was doing something wrong, so I took it personally. Over the years I have learned that people are going to leave no matter what you do. You simply can't please everyone. Don't take it personally when someone leaves…it's just a part of ministry.

Remember God is at work. In every situation, God is at work. He may be building the ministry by removing people who are standing in the way of future growth. He may want to do a new work in the lives that are leaving. Many times he will use the situation to bring you into a closer relationship with him.

Let them go. In my early years of ministry, I would try to keep people from leaving. I would try to talk them into staying, write notes of encouragement, and invest even more hours into the relationship.

One day I sat down with the pastor of one of the largest churches in America. I asked him what he did when people decided to leave his church. I thought he would give me a plan on how to keep them from leaving. His response was, "Just let them go."

I learned a valuable lesson that day. When someone decides to leave, there is usually nothing you can do. Don't try to stop them. They need to find a church where they can be happy. They need to find a church where they can wholeheartedly support the vision and philosophy. Don't try to stand in their way.

Wish them well. Part ways with a smile. Don't let anger or bitterness creep in. You don't want to get to the point where you are avoiding them in the store six months down the road. Let them know you love them and nothing will change that. Remember the good times you had with them.

Learn from them. Normally when someone is getting ready to leave, you'll hear the famous words "we need to talk." Usually they've already decided to leave. Use the conversation to learn and grow. Ask about areas where you could have helped them more. If they have complaints, listen carefully. If they're leaving because of a legitimate offense, apologize and seek to make things right. If they're leaving because of a mistake you made, then learn from it and use it as a catalyst for personal growth.

Rally those who remain around the mission. I believe it's important to periodically call people back to your mission. Remind those who remain why you exist as a ministry or team. Cast vision for the future. Let them know the best days are ahead.

Replace them. The most important thing you can do is replace the person who has left. So a family left—go reach a new family for Christ. So a volunteer quit—go recruit three new volunteers. Spend your time and energy on those God is bringing in, not on those who are leaving. New faces will bring new life to a ministry or team that is hurting from someone leaving.

People will walk away. How you wave goodbye will affect your ministry.

—**Dale**

22

Honey, It's Gonna Get Better

In nearly six years of ministry, I've made a few mistakes. (OK, *lots* of mistakes.) I learned from some of them. Others, I had to repeat a few times. One of my biggest mistakes was communicating poorly with my wife in one specific area: how our ministry was going to affect my life and our family. When writing to the church at Corinth, Paul said:

"I want you to be free from the concerns of this life. An unmarried man can spend his time doing the Lord's work and thinking how to please him. But a married man has to think about his earthly responsibilities and how to please his wife. His interests are divided. In the same way, a woman who is no longer married or has never been married can be devoted to the Lord and holy in body and in spirit. But a married woman has to think about her earthly responsibilities and how to please her husband" (1 Corinthians 7:32-34).

Wait a minute, Scott! Are you saying ministry comes before family? No, I'm quoting Paul. *Then are you saying that family hinders you from ministry?* Yes, and I'm still quoting Paul. Should ministry be a priority over family? That's a difficult question, both to ask and to answer. Serving the Lord and obeying his call should supersede everything else in our lives. I know from experience that sometimes that means family. Before you get upset with me, read a little farther in that same passage. Paul goes on to say that he and those who were unmarried should remain that way, devoting themselves wholly to the Lord. He also acknowledged that most people choose marriage. So you're married, and you're in ministry. Well, have fun with that. (I know I have.) But don't be dumb.

Don't apologize, and don't lie...even unintentionally. In the early days of my ministry, I apologized constantly. I kept telling my wife, "Honey, it's gonna get better." By saying this, I was implying that "someday" the work would be done. The ministry would be built. I'd be surrounded by droves of people at my beck and call, and life would be grand...just "not yet." Guess what? Not ever. It never ends, unless you die or your ministry is already dead. It never stops, unless you quit growing or are removed from your role. There are never enough people to get everything done. That's OK. Just don't "accidentally" lie to your family. I'd say it with each new season. I'd felt guilty for saying it, and often even for continuing the work. My justifications disappointed her, disappointed myself, and most likely saddened the Lord.

There is no balance. Grow to cope. There's no real balance in ministry. My pastor vehemently protects his Fridays with his family, and his date night with his wife. Then he has to leave them alone without him all weekend, every weekend. He has not been able to sit with his wife in church consistently for more than 10 years. That's not balance; it's compromise. But not in a bad way. It's reality. Work hard to help your family share your belief in what you do and your confidence in why you do it.

Your family needs you. Help them understand by being honest with them. Help them understand by setting boundaries and sticking to them. Help them understand and support you by taking intentional time away from everything else to focus exclusively on them. Recently, my 11-year-old son and I were talking. I asked him how he was feeling about all that was happening in our ministry. He said, "Dad, I'm so proud of everything we've accomplished." It was never only my calling, only my sacrifice, only my life. It doesn't get better than that moment.

—Scott

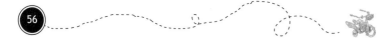

23

Yo' Momma!

Parents are the primary spiritual influence for their children—either positively or negatively. That's why it's so important to intentionally reach out to parents who are not Christ-followers. Effective ministry not only impacts the child, but the parents as well.

My family is a great example of this. In past generations, we were far from God. In fact, my great-grandfather made and sold illegal alcohol. He was a violent man and killed a man in the front yard of his house while my father watched as a little boy. He was sent to prison.

My grandfather followed in his footsteps and was violent and abusive. Holidays were filled with fighting and drunkenness. We knew nothing of God.

Then one day something happened that would change the course of our family. A man in the neighborhood stopped by and asked my family to go to church. At first they said no, but the man keep coming by and asking. Finally my grandmother and father went. My father walked into church for the first time as a little boy and heard of Jesus' love.

My father and grandmother became Christ-followers. My father began preaching at age 15. His greatest burden was for his father, who was still far from God. He kept asking my grandfather to come to church. Finally, one day he came to hear my father speak. That day God came down and touched my grandfather's heart. He was changed. The fighting and drunkenness stopped. Peace entered the home. My grandfather became a man who served for many years as a deacon before he passed away just a few years ago. God turned our family around. Now there are four ministers in our family: my father, Van Hudson, who is a pastor; my brother, Devin, who is a pastor; my brother, Derek, who is a worship leader; and myself, a children's pastor. Our family was changed forever!

IDEAS

- Invite parents to come see their child perform or be part of a program. If a child is performing, singing, or is part of a program, parents will come. Strategically plan for this. Share the gospel at these opportunities in an appropriate way.

- Require parents to attend the children's new believers class with their child. They will hear the gospel as their child hears it...and many of them will step across the line of faith with their child. I have seen it happen time and again. Recently we baptized seven parents as a direct result of them attending a new believers class with their children. God worked in their hearts as they sat through the class.

- Build relationships with parents. Get to know the parents of the kids in your ministry. Many times the only reason we approach them is to ask for something. How about connecting with them with the purpose of building a relationship that leads to a better partnership?

> Reach a child and you change a life. Reach the parents and you change the entire family.

- Have an open house and invite parents to come and observe their child's environment in action. This will help them feel the heartbeat of the ministry, which will lead to the desire to partner with you.

- Partner with parents. What if you asked parents how you could partner with them in their child's spiritual development? What if you asked what their child's biggest need is and how they could help meet it? What if you asked how you could pray for the child?

- Provide a parent website. The website could contain audio of the children's weekend lesson along with discussion questions. It could also contain helpful Scripture, articles, and parenting tips for every stage of child development. (See Idea 77 for more information about a parent website.)

- Provide or recommend tools and resources. Provide a list of recommended children's Bibles, devotion books, and parenting resources. If you have a bookstore in your church, request that the items you recommend stay in stock.

And never underestimate the power of prayer. Years ago at a new church plant in California, there lived a man a few doors down. He was an ex-gang member and had a history of violence and criminal activities. I invited him to church and he quickly told me that he had never been to church, was an atheist, and wanted no part of God.

That father went on to become a minister and has personally brought hundreds of people to Christ. I talked to him recently and he is still passionately following Christ.

A family that was reached…a family that now has hope…a family that has been changed forever! (Want to hear how it happened? Turn to Idea 99, When Kids Pray!)

—**Dale**

Have you ever been accosted by a furious parent? I have. Here's what's funny (kind of): Nine out of 10 of these interactions invoke two names: Jesus and Craig. They inform me what Jesus would do and what my pastor would think. I just smile (most of the time) and try to produce a workable solution.

Here's a case in point:

Change what needs to be changed. A few years ago we changed the policy for our evening discipleship program, KONNECT. After visiting Saddleback Church in Orange County and seeing their model for discipleship and how they accomplish it in a church with thousands of children, we knew it was time for a change. So change we did.

The following fall, we required that every child in attendance be registered. This meant that their parents had to meet a few simple requirements: They had to (1) attend an informational meeting, (2) commit to partner with us in their home, (3) pay a small fee (scholarships were available based on need), and (4) commit to being there as many of the 28 weeks as they could by making KONNECT a priority in their lives and in the lives of their children.

We knew that these changes would be tough, especially at the beginning. But we were running out of space and volunteers. We weren't providing excellence, which is one of our core values. We needed to temporarily drop our numbers so we could increase our excellence over time.

Communicate, communicate, communicate. To communicate the change, we did everything we could think of. We put announcements in the bulletin every week for months, we handed out fliers to parents as they picked up their children, we ran advertisements in "big church," we had a splash on the website, we sent mailers to everyone whose address we could get, we talked about it, we sang about it, and we performed dramas that reinforced the spirit of the change. (OK, maybe those last two are an exaggeration. But just barely.)

We did everything we reasonably could. To accommodate parents, we offered multiple sign-up events, on different days and at different times. We offered scholarships for those in need. We communicated through the small-group department. And yet, when the fall semester arrived, some parents—quite a few, actually—showed up to drop off their kids and were furious! "How could you turn away a child? What kind of children's 'ministry' are you running here?"

Clearly define your ministries. Every weekend in the course of normal ministry, we offer between three and seven experiences for kids, depending on which campus they attend. (That's more than 40 total.) We have never—since I've been the children's pastor—"closed a room" due to the high number in attendance. All are welcome, every time.

But KONNECT is different. It's not evangelism. It's discipleship. It's about the same adult being with the same eight kids every weekend. It's about consistency. It's about forming lifelong habits of worship and study. It's about partnering with parents, providing them with the tools to do in the home that which is their responsibility and gift—and which we cannot do in two hours a week. It's about commitment. It's about loyalty. It's about the cumulative benefit of 28 weeks per year where experiences build upon each other.

Persevere. The end result has been (and continues to emerge as) a success. Our numbers initially dropped, just as we expected, but then gradually increased to exceed our previous highs.

We learned that, as a general rule, when parents pay a small fee for something, they value it more than if it were free. We learned that kids want to be a part of something big, and they ask to come back. We see relationships grow, flourish, and continue as they leave our ministry in the transition into the youth program.

We've been doing KONNECT for four years now. Yes, parents *still* show up angry each year, even after they've ignored all the information we've provided. And they tell us what Jesus and Pastor Craig would do.

(But that's OK.)

—**Scott**

The Return of the Guest!

Our church is located in one of the fastest-growing cities in America. The metro population of Las Vegas in 1980 was a little over 400,000. At the time of this writing, it's closing in on 2,000,000. Every month 7,000 new residents move into our valley.

As a church, it's awesome to be in such a growing city. Each weekend dozens of new families walk through our doors for the very first time. On some weekends it can be as many as 200 new families visiting for the first time. Lack of first-time guests is not a problem.

The greatest questions we face are "How do we get them to come back after their first visit?" "How do we get them connected so they can become followers of Christ?" "How can we help them become a part of our church family?"

Here are some things we're doing to answer these questions and to ensure "The Return of the Guest."

Make sure they have a great first experience. Have you ever had a bad experience at a business or restaurant? I have, and I'm sure you can think of a few as well. Now every time you ride by that store or restaurant, you remember the bad experience.

I believe the number-one factor in seeing your guests return is to give them a great first experience. Here's the deal…plain and simple. Knock it out of the ballpark with them on their first visit. Make that first visit one they'll never forget. Turn to Idea 7 for ideas to get you started in providing a great experience. Then read on for more.

Follow up. Follow up within two days of their visit. If you wait more than two days, you're diminishing the chances for return. Send a letter to the parents. Thank them for being your guests, and say you'd love to partner with them in their child's spiritual journey.

Try a survey. In the letter, invite the parents to take an online survey about their first visit. (If you choose, let them know at the end of the survey there will be a coupon they can print out for a free gift from your church. The gift can be anything from a free cup of coffee to a book on their next visit.) Online surveys can be set up fairly inexpensively and are a great way to get feedback. They also make guests feel valued that you would ask for their input and ideas. We use zoomerang.com.

Here are the questions we ask:

1. Which service did you attend?
2. Were you greeted with a smile?
3. Were you personally walked to your child's age-specific environment (room)?
4. Were the room leaders who greeted you friendly, and did they answer any questions you had?
5. Provide any additional information/suggestions to help increase our friendliness factor.
6. Was our safety and security process explained to you and followed? (Rate 1 to 10.)
7. Did you feel your child was safe? (Rate 1 to 10.)
8. Was your security badge checked as you left the room?
9. Please provide any additional information/suggestions to help our safety and security process.
10. Was your child's environment clean and presentable? (Rate 1 to 10.)
11. Did your child have fun? (Rate 1 to 10.)
12. Did your child enjoy the environment? (Rate 1 to 10.)
13. Please provide any specific feedback about your child's environment.

We have found this online survey to be invaluable. It's a great way to get ideas on how you can improve, and many times it's a great source of encouragement you can pass along to your team.

Send a handwritten note to the child. In the day of flashy brochures and high-tech marketing, this will make the child feel special and will add a great personal touch. Enclose it with the parent letter, and address the envelope to the parent. This shows the parent again that you would like to partner with him or her.

Make a brief phone call to the family. The phone call should not be pushy. Simply thank them for coming and see if they have any questions you can answer. For us, a brief call is much more effective than trying to visit their home. We have also found that if a volunteer makes the call, it makes a bigger impact than a staff member calling.

Look for ways to connect. If your guests didn't come with someone who attends your church, look for opportunities to connect them with someone who is already a part of your church. This could be someone who lives near them, has children the same ages, or is a part of a class they attended.

Do all the guests who walk through our doors return? No. But many do, and we are able to help them get connected with Christ.

Each new child…each new family that walks through your doors is valuable to God. God has sent them to you. He is working in their lives, and he is reaching out to them through you. Open your arms. Let them feel God's love through your words, your actions, your smile, your kindness, and your hospitality. Let them leave without any doubt in their minds that there *is* something real to this God thing. Do that, and you will often experience "The Return of the Guest!"

—**Dale**

26

Kids Can't Drive

Our church has grown from around 400 people in its first year, when my wife and I first began attending, to more than 25,000 people every weekend now. We've grown from three services at a single location to over 40 weekend worship experiences in six states at 11 campuses. Through my pastor's vision and leadership—and God's blessing—the last 10 years have exceeded our every dream. Maybe you're about to add your second service, or maybe you're about to add your 10th campus. It doesn't matter. The same rules apply. And the earlier you can institute them, the better off you'll be. It all comes down to consistency.

Fact: Kids can't drive. (Well, not legally or safely, anyway.) That means, with few exceptions, kids' parents decide when (or if) they come to church. That decision may be influenced by worship styles, programs offered, and so on. In our church, we attempt to offer the same experience at every service throughout a weekend. And in each experience, we strive for excellence.

If it's not good for every child, it's not good for any of them. People have some great ideas. Fantastic ideas, even. They've often come to me wanting to do something in the kids ministry. One offered to bring in live animals. Another offered to incorporate dance as a part of a series I was teaching on worship. Many have offered to perform live music. As we grew, adding more services and more campuses, that created a dilemma. The people who wanted to do their special thing rarely (if ever) wanted to do it *eight times* on *two different campuses*, starting at 5:00 p.m. on Saturday and finishing at 8:00 p.m. on Sunday.

Through video, and through clearly defining volunteer roles on campuses, we settled on a system that worked for us, for everybody. You can, too. A few people were mad when we politely turned them down. A few people had hurt feelings. We had to give up some things we loved because they simply wouldn't translate to video, or because we couldn't duplicate them at all the different campus sizes and locations.

But when you walk into our children's ministry, whether you're in Fort Worth, Texas; West Palm Beach, Florida; or Stillwater, Oklahoma; you get the same thing. Whether you go on a Saturday night, early on a Sunday morning, or in the middle of Sunday afternoon, you get all the excellence we have to offer. Our kids deserve that. Your guests deserve that. Excellence demands it.

'Cause guess what? Kids can't drive.

—**Scott**

27

Money Speaks Louder Than Words!
(What's Your Budget Saying?)

> "Wherever your treasure is, there the desires of your heart will also be."
>
> —Matthew 6:21

Your children's ministry budget reflects what's important to you. How you spend your budget shows where your priorities lie. Your requests for additional funds for special projects indicate what your passion is.

Let's be honest. All of us need more money for our ministries. I've never heard anyone say, "My budget is too big. I don't know how to spend all the money." If you are aggressively seeking to reach kids and families in your community, you will always be looking for additional funding.

But no matter the size of your budget, you can put it to work to help you fulfill God's plan for your children's ministry. The issue is not the amount of money in your budget, but what you do with it. Here are three simple steps to help you maximize the budget God has entrusted you with.

Write your mission statement. What is the purpose of your children's ministry? Where are you seeking to lead people? What do you want to see God do in people's lives through your children's ministry? What do you want kids and families to know, be, and do?

IDEAS

- Remember ministry is about people…plain and simple. Make sure your budget says one thing: people.
- Your children's ministry mission should be in sync with the overall mission of your church. Mission that is aligned is powerful and effective.

Create a plan that will help fulfill your mission. The plan should consist of strategic steps that make the mission happen. Here's an example. Central Kidz's mission is "Connecting kids and families to Christ and helping them become followers of him." Our plan is made up of strategic steps for people to follow, such as attending weekend services, going through a new believers class, getting baptized, participating in a spiritual growth campaign, joining a small group, being part of a service project, and so on.

IDEAS

- The steps of your plan should be simple and clear. Make it easy for people to know the next step on the pathway.

- Evaluate and make sure all your steps are effective. If steps are not effectively fulfilling the mission, then drop or adjust them. Don't spend your budget money on steps that aren't working.

Budget your steps. You've written down your mission. You've designed a plan made up of strategic steps to help fulfill the mission. Now allocate your budget to those steps. Of course, there are line items like office supplies that will not be directly tied to a specific step, but the vast majority of your budget should be directly funding a step.

Is reaching out to new families important to you? Then make sure your budget reflects it. Is discipling kids a part of your mission? Then your budget should be yelling that loud and clear.

Money speaks louder than words. What is your budget saying?

—Dale

28

Let's Do Lunch

How long have you been in ministry? One week? One decade? Either way, sometime in the past (or maybe even right now), you've probably felt lonely or isolated and desired to be understood or a part of a team. I found a great way to fight those "all alone" blues. Even better, the same remedy also helped me build lasting relationships that became vital to our success and longevity as a ministry. It will work for you, too.

Find strength in numbers. When I first took the job as children's pastor, I knew *nothing*. I had zero experience in this field, but my pastor entrusted me with the job, and I knew that God had called me to do it. Drawing on my business experience, I knew that I could only succeed if I could network; I needed to model myself after other successful individuals. So I began looking for ways to do that in ministry.

The approach that God blessed the most was starting a community Children's Ministry Luncheon. I fondly remember the first time we met. Five or six people attended, and none of us knew each other. Now, years later, these same people are not only my friends, but they're some of my most trusted allies. I'm incredibly grateful for the source of support and encouragement they have all become. If you can find such a gathering where you live and work, get involved. If there's not one, start one! Read on for how-to instructions.

Put yourself out there. Use the phone book, Internet, and advice of your church staff to compile a list of possible attendees. Then make a spreadsheet mailing list. While you're making it, keep in mind that this same file will make a good sign-in sheet that you can use at your first luncheon, and lay it out accordingly. Use a small, simple postcard for your invitations. For your first mailing, you might want to write a short letter of introduction. Explain (briefly!) what you're trying to do. Share your heart, and be humble. Then watch what God does. This group may become one of the most important communities in your life.

Pay attention to the details. Here are a few practical tips to keep in mind as you're planning.

- *Select a location.* We rotate our luncheon to a different location monthly. Host the first one at your church. Restaurants can work for smaller groups, but they're loud, which makes it difficult to carry on meaningful conversation and it can be hard to keep everyone involved. If you do use a public place, request a private room.

- *Send invitations.* Mail your invitations two weeks before the event. Be sure to ask for an R.S.V.P. to your e-mail or phone. "Snail mail" is the best way to invite people for the first six months or so. Over time, you'll probably be able to switch to e-mail coordination.

- *Arrange for food in advance.* Have the hosting party provide drinks and paper goods, and have the food brought in (pizza or box lunches are fine), charging a nominal amount per participant (usually around $5 to $7).

- *Use name tags.* Have blank name tags laid out with markers. As you're asking people to sign in, also ask them to write what they want to be called and where they minister. This will be critical to helping everyone get acquainted. It also makes introductions easier and less awkward.

- *Start with prayer.* Once you have everyone seated, thank them all for coming, and ask if you can briefly pray. Thank God for the privilege of meeting together across denominational lines, ministry styles, and geographical areas for a common goal.

- *You invited…so lead (at least at first).* Be prepared to facilitate discussion. For the benefit of new guests, introduce yourself each time you meet. Explain why the group exists and what you hope everyone will get out of it. Your first meeting can be used to explore topics of interest for future meetings, but be sure you have a topic to discuss at this meeting, as well. You might ask participants what their greatest ministry challenges are, or ask people to share their best advice for getting volunteers or doing outreach.

- *Ask for help.* As your meetings evolve into a regular event, solicit others in the group to help you with mailings, planning, record keeping, and any other administrative tasks. Remember, this is not your thing. You may have been the organizer, but it belongs to the group and to the Lord.

- *Take a tour.* When the luncheon is being hosted by a ministry at a church, ask them to kick off your meeting with a brief tour of their facility. No matter how big or small, it's great to see what God is doing in different places. We usually do this in groups at the beginning and then gather for lunch after the groups have toured.

- *Use the list.* We often send e-mails to the whole group when one of us has an opening, an opportunity, or a need. It's remarkable how valuable this resource has become over time.

Expect to be blessed! These are people who know what you do, how hard you work, and the blessings that accompany ministering to children. It will be like few other communities you can be a part of.

—**Scott**

29

The Song That Never Ends!

"And you must commit yourselves wholeheartedly to these commands that I am giving you today. Repeat them again and again to your children."

—Deuteronomy 6:6-7a

Somewhere, sometime long ago, someone decided to create a song to inflict cruel and unusual punishment on adults. The song is rightly called "The Song That Never Ends." It's a simple song that repeats the same lines over and over and over and over and over. If you've been in children's ministry for very long, you've probably heard it. I have endured the song on many a bus trip to camp. It goes on and on until finally an adult on the brink of insanity puts a stop to it.

I must admit the song is embedded in my memory forever. Whoever wrote it should get credit for knowing one thing for sure—if you want something to be remembered forever, then use repetition! It's the key to something becoming a permanent part of you.

Let's stop and ask ourselves this question. Can the kids we teach recall the truths we have taught them as well as "The Song That Never Ends"? Have we embedded the truth of God's Word in their hearts, minds, and souls that well? If we're going to see it happen, then we must put the teaching mode on loop.

Over the course of several years, we've made a shift to a repetitive teaching loop. We've seen amazing results as the truth becomes embedded in kids' hearts, minds, and souls. Here are some of the key principles that guide us.

Teach a core set of simple, essential truths. Decide as a team what you want kids to know and live out when they leave your ministry. What are the "must know" truths? List those truths, and focus your teaching on them. The 52 weeks in a year go by fast. You've only got 52 opportunities to embed eternal truth into kids' lives each year. And let's be honest, the number is probably about half that. Most families attend church twice a month or even less. Add in divorce and joint-custody situations, and your teaching opportunities in a year aren't that many.

It's vital to zoom in on a core set of simple, essential truths to teach. Make each truth a simple, short statement that is easy to say and remember. An example is "God has a special plan for my life."

Turn each truth you teach into a series that lasts four weeks. Teach the same core truth for those weeks using a different Bible story or lesson each week to illustrate it.

Make sure kids remember and understand one key verse for each series. The key verse should be the foundation of the truth you are teaching.

Repeat, repeat, repeat, repeat, repeat, and repeat some more! Repetition accelerates retention. According to Thom and Joani Schultz in their book *The Dirt on Learning*, if you hear something one time in a month, you remember less than 10 percent of it. If you hear something six times in a month, your retention rate goes to 90 percent! Think of the results when you take one key truth and repeat it over and over with kids during a month. They'll never forget it!

Use every part of the service to reinforce the key truth. Strategically plan every element of your service to emphasize the truth you're teaching. Don't just have a game for the sake of having a game; have a game that illustrates your core truth. Don't just do a skit about a random idea; do a skit that shows the core teaching truth being lived out in everyday life.

IDEAS

- Pick a theme song for the series that goes along with your core teaching truth. Sing that song every week during the series for one of your song elements.

- Have a review game at the end of each session that reinforces the truth they have learned.

Have everyone study the same core truths. Do you want to see your retention rate go off the charts? Then have all age-specific ministries commit to teaching the same core truths. Partner with parents by communicating to them your key teaching truths. You could also make a wall sign that shows your core teaching truths. Post a sign in each environment for all to see. This will bring great clarity and vision to your team, parents, and the kids.

Recently we had a fifth-grade graduation celebration to honor our kids who were moving into junior high ministry. I sat back in tears and listened as they shared their testimonies. I could hear the core truths echoing out of their hearts and souls. I pray they eat, sleep, dream, breathe, and live those truths for the rest of their lives!

—**Dale**

Mr. Catfish

Walk into the 1:00 p.m. experience at our largest campus. Proceed directly to the Guest Services counter. Tell them you're my guest. Complete the form for a Guest Pass. Go into Toon Town and find a large group of kids surrounding a guy in a hat. Read his name tag: Mr. Catfish. Yes, you read that correctly: Mr. Catfish. It's his nickname. It has been for years. Most people don't know his real name. (I do, but I'm not telling.)

The point is, we encourage men to serve in our ministry. And we try to make it as much fun for them as for the kids. Your name tag can read "Mr. Catfish," "The Boz," "Iguana," whatever you want it to (within reason). We know who you are! Have fun! Enjoy yourself. Enjoy the kids.

Men are servants, too. One thing that sets us apart from other ministries is that we have a lot of guys. Seriously…a lot. Somewhere between one-third and one-half of our more than 500 weekly Cast Members (volunteers) are men. We have men of all ages. We have Junior Cast Members, school-aged young people who worship during one experience and serve during another each weekend. We have parents. We have college students. We have senior citizens. That's no happy accident. We identified and created roles where men love to serve, and they show up week after week, ready to go.

No such thing as a liability. Men are not allowed to change diapers. Not my rule. It's a rule of our insurance carrier. Is it sexist? Yeah, it is. Should it be a rule? Maybe not. Does that matter? No—it's a rule, and there's nothing we can do about it. So why fight it? We broadcast it! We advertise it! *"Wanna be a rock(ing chair) star? Love to hold babies? Bring it on! And guess what, guys? You're not allowed to change poopy, stinky diapers!"* They love it. We've turned a rule, a liability, into a marketing tool and recruiting advantage for guys who love babies.

In addition, we won't open a room without two volunteers present. We don't want any volunteer to be alone with a child, at any time, for any reason.

This protection allows men the freedom to serve without the fear of false accusations.

Enjoy serving. We like fun. We slime kids, shove pies in their faces, make them drink blended-up Happy Meals, make them wear pantyhose over their heads. Show me a guy who doesn't love that stuff.

Just show up. You know what you have to do to serve for us? Show up. That's not every role, of course. But many of our roles require nothing more than to show up and love kids. That's entirely on purpose on our part. Most guys aren't likely to do three hours of prep time during the week. So we make serving easy by providing everything they'll need.

Cast Members can connect with children in a way that will not only point kids toward a relationship with Jesus Christ, but also change their own hearts.

We deliberately created policies and the environments where guys love to serve. They bring their buddies, they show up, and they do a great job every week. You can do that, too.

Maybe you could have your very own Mr. Catfish.

—**Scott**

Mustard Seeds, Fishing Nets, and Toys!

> "Here is another illustration Jesus used: 'The Kingdom of Heaven is like a mustard seed planted in a field.' "
>
> —Matthew 13:31

> "Again, the Kingdom of Heaven is like a fishing net that was thrown into the water and caught fish of every kind."
>
> —Matthew 13:47

Jesus connected people to his eternal truth by using ordinary, everyday objects from their culture. In the above verses, we see two examples. If you follow this cue from Jesus, you will help kids connect to your teaching in an amazing way. Here are some ways to make it happen.

Use items from current kid culture to illustrate your teaching. We recently did a series about growing in your faith. We wanted to help kids get to the next level in their relationships with Jesus. We looked into kid culture for ideas. We realized that nearly every day kids try to get to the next level in the video games they play. We found it to be a perfect way to illustrate going to the next level with Jesus. We tied our lessons, activities, games, and small-group discussions to getting to the next level in a video game. The kids immediately connected. Our prayer is that now every time they pick up a video game controller, it will be a reminder to go to the next level in their relationships with Jesus.

Use ordinary objects that kids see or come in contact with to illustrate your teaching. Make a list of ordinary objects that kids regularly come in contact with—objects like backpacks, bikes, sandwiches, pillows, chairs, gum, tennis shoes, and soccer balls. Always have an object in hand. Since many kids are visual learners, showing the object instead of just talking about it is much more effective.

Use animals that kids are familiar with to illustrate your teaching. Jesus talked about birds, snakes, worms, moths, sheep, wolves, and more.

Kids love animals and are naturally curious about them. That's why going to the zoo is such an exciting experience for kids. A few years ago, I did a teaching series called "Animals of the Bible." Each week we used a live animal to illustrate a lesson. One week we had a pig (prodigal son), another week we had a snake (temptation in the garden), and another week we had a rooster (Peter's denial).

The final week's lesson was on Daniel and the lions' den. I decided to make it a lesson that the kids would never forget. When the kids came in, there was a huge cage on stage covered by a tarp. When I got to the part about Daniel being thrown in the lions' den, we pulled the tarp back and sure enough…there was a real lion pacing back and forth. He let out a roar and the lesson came to life for the kids! I had connected with a local zoo, and they had brought the lion and cage.

IDEAS

- Check with people in your church when looking for animals. Farmers or people who work at local animal shelters are a great source.

- Check with local zoos. Many times they will bring an animal for a free show.

- Check with local pet stores. They may be willing to come and show their animals and insects. (It's free advertising for them.)

- If you can't secure a live insect or animal, then use a picture of it as a last resort.

- Always make sure safety is your top priority when bringing in live animals and insects. A child being bitten would most definitely ruin your lesson!

Repeat the truths in daily life. Deuteronomy 6:4-9 reminds us that we should talk about God's truths with kids throughout the day. At home, in the car, at the grocery store, at the ball field, wherever we are. Here's an example.

I was driving our fourth- and fifth-graders to an activity. Suddenly from the back of the bus, a fifth-grade boy yelled out, "Hey, Dale! Look! A one-way sign! There is only one way to heaven…it's Jesus!" I was amazed. A year earlier we had had a lesson on Jesus being the one and only way to heaven. I had used a one-way traffic sign when I taught the lesson. Just an ordinary object that a kid might see every day. That sign helped him grasp the truth.

Now for the rest of his life, when he rides down the road and sees a one-way sign, he's going to be reminded that Jesus is the one and only way to heaven.

So grab some toys, some movie clips, some animals, some objects or items from a kid's world—and watch your teaching go to a new level!

—**Dale**

32

Never Give Up. Never Surrender.

Have you ever seen the movie *Galaxy Quest?* If you haven't, you should rent it sometime. It absolutely will…not change your life. But it will probably make you smile.

The way the quirky characters in this movie bumble their way through their mission reminds me of a senior pastor and a youth guy. One of my dearest friends introduced me to this film when we were traveling together, and it showed on the airplane we were on. We enjoyed it together, literally laughing out loud, time after time. Maybe we were just tired. (Maybe we're just stupid.) Regardless, we had fun and created a memory that we both enjoy to this day.

The characters' catch phrase? "Never give up. Never surrender."

Do you ever feel like quitting? Have you ever just wanted to throw in the towel? Have you ever been so empty inside that you felt like you had nothing left to give? You're not alone.

The characters in *Galaxy Quest* encountered grotesque aliens—perhaps not unlike your finance director. They faced huge obstacles—comparable to staff meetings. They overcame unbeatable odds—like your budget. How did they persist? They lived their mantra: "Never give up. Never surrender." Here are a few tips to keep you strong.

Welcome to ministry. The honeymoon's over. Ministry's hard. Maybe you once held an idealistic vision, one where a group of hyper-spiritual beings sit around a campfire together singing "Kumbaya." Your first staff meeting should have killed that. If not, then surely your first irate parent calling dumped ice water on you. Either way, welcome to ministry. (Actually, welcome to life.) In ministry, just as in any other setting, we're surrounded by people, and people are inherently flawed. Even you.

Don't tire of doing good. When the finance alien's about to disintegrate you, take heart. Never give up. Never surrender. If it seems like no one's listening, never give up. Never surrender. When the trapdoor snaps shut in front of you, and it's clear your vision won't survive, never give up. Never surrender.

In his letter to Galatians, Paul put it like this: "Let's not get tired of doing what is good. At just the right time we will reap a harvest of blessing if we don't give up" (6:9).

Rent a funny movie. Remind yourself how to laugh again. Remember, people are people. They'll make mistakes. (Include yourself in that.) But never forget your purpose. Never forget your calling. Never forget the result awaiting all who persevere.

Never give up! Never surrender!

—Scott

33

Kids Say the Coolest Things!

I was visiting a family that had recently started attending our church. They had come regularly but then missed a few weeks. I went to see how they were. The mom began to tell me they had been missing church due to her husband being on business trips. Her son was listening to our conversation and motioned for me to come close. I bent down, and he whispered in my ear, "Daddy's in jail." He had cut straight to the truth. Needless to say, Mom was pretty embarrassed.

I love talking with kids. Their simple, genuine conversation is so refreshing. Kids will normally open up and share their hearts with you when approached properly. Here are some effective ways to talk with kids.

Get on their level. Kneel or sit down so you can have direct eye contact with them. This will communicate that you want to talk *with* them instead of down to them.

Call them by name. When you call a child by name, it shows that he or she is important to you. If you have a large number of children in your ministry and haven't memorized all their names yet, then make sure all the kids wear name tags. This allows you to call each child by name.

Communicate acceptance. Say something that lets them know you think they are great. Phrases such as "What's up, cool dude," "How's the most awesome girl in the world doing?" "Billy is in the house," and "Hey, it's great to see you" show kids you accept them and care about them. High fives are also a great way to communicate acceptance.

Talk about their world. Be knowledgeable about kids' toys, video games, websites, movies, music, sports, and school. This can give you an instant connection with them. There is a boy who attends our church. He smiles and talks with me often. It wasn't that way the first time I met him. He was sitting in the back of the room with a scowl on his face. I went back and sat down on the floor beside him. When I started talking about the latest video games, his face immediately lit up. He couldn't believe an "old guy" like me knew about the video games he played. I had entered his world and connected with him.

Swap jokes. Kids love jokes. They love to hear and tell them. Try it next time you're talking with a kid. He or she will respond. I like swapping "knock-knock" jokes with kids. Don't worry about the joke being corny. The sillier, the better.

Ask open-ended questions. Move beyond simple yes-or-no questions. Ask questions that will get kids talking. Use questions such as "What was the coolest thing you did this week?" "How are things going at school?" and "How did your soccer game turn out yesterday?"

Listen to them. There are times when it *looks* like we're listening but we're not really tuned in. Slow down and hit pause on the "to-do list" that's running through your mind. If necessary, silently repeat to yourself what the child is saying so you can stay focused. Ask the child questions about what's been said to show you're tuned in.

Jesus took time to talk with children. The disciples tried to chase them away, but Jesus basically said, "Hang on a minute. These kids are important. I want to talk with them!" He took them into his arms and blessed them. Jesus still wants to do that today. He wants to speak words of kindness to them through your voice. He wants to listen to the details of their lives through your ears. He wants them to see his love as they look into your eyes. Will you do it?

—**Dale**

Never Let Them See You Sweat

Over the years, our team has incorporated several sayings into our culture:

Go big or go home.

Stick with me…I'm going somewhere.

If it's worth doing, it's worth doing right.

We have many, many more. And one of my personal favorites, one I'm sure my team is sick of hearing from me, is this:

Never let them see you sweat.

I may have mentioned this once or twice before: One of my favorite organizations is Disney. Not everything they do, of course, and not a lot of the business decisions they make. Mainly I just love Walt—what he stood for and what he achieved. Here are a few things I've learned from one of the best.

Hide the machinery. One fundamental concept that has contributed to Disney's success is "the stage." The parks themselves are actually networked with hidden passageways—tunnels and corridors that the public never sees. These catacombs exist for the sole purpose of moving cast members from point A to point B, maintaining the illusion. Passages are clearly marked as "backstage" or "onstage" to avoid confusion for cast members. Anything within public view is "onstage." I love that concept. You'll never see a Disney character sitting at a corn dog stand, smoking a Marlboro, his feet propped on his mascot head under the table. They preserve the magic. They remember that people may have waited their whole lives for this day.

We ministers can learn so much from the hard work Disney's already done for us, both literally and figuratively. On our team we call realizations "ah-ha moments." "Never let them see you sweat" was an ah-ha for us. Here's what it means: You're here for a reason. This is not about you. From the time you cross the threshold to the time you get back in your car, remain on task, smile, and operate in the confidence of your calling, firm in the knowledge that you are prepared.

Here's how we make that work in practical terms.

Leave your issues in the parking lot. Can you imagine walking your daughter up to Snow White, and Snow White starts talking about the horrible week she's had? When you're serving, you're here to minister to others. Save your issues for a more appropriate time, your best friend, your accountability partner, your small group, your counselor. Children's ministry is not the time or place.

Smile. Your demeanor often sets the tone for the volunteers on duty. If you're hurried and chaotic, watch: It will infect others. They will respond to your mood. If you're upbeat, friendly, and cheerful, you'll feel it back in the halls!

Lay down your cross. Have you ever met that staff person who just loves to let you know how tired he is, or just how much she's sacrificing to do the job? These exchanges are often so uncomfortable they make volunteers feel guilty. Fact: The very people for whom you're playing the martyr worked somewhere else all week, and they're not getting paid for this gig. Ministry is a blessing. As Paul described, learn to be content in all things. God knows your sacrifice. That's all that matters.

Don't procrastinate. Never put off anything until the weekend that can be done before. Surprises are inevitable. Things go wrong. Someone doesn't show; some parents need to visit with you before they're comfortable dropping off their child; cleanup on aisle 3! The main secret to pulling off a successful event is this: Do everything you possibly can before the day of the event. It makes a huge difference.

The 3-minute rule. Except in the case of an emergency, during weekend sessions never get into a conversation with a parent or volunteer that lasts more than three minutes. Call them or e-mail them later, if necessary. Don't squander your opportunity to have contact with the 20 families that will walk past you while you're talking to someone else. You have a job to do.

This isn't easy. We had to train for it. Teach your staff to truthfully explain: "I really care about you. I want to help you with this, and I'd love to visit with you later. I'll be done here at _____ o'clock. Can you come back then? If that won't work for you, let's meet on _____ (day) at _____ (time) this week. If you need help right this minute, I can introduce you to a member of our pastoral staff."

Be the expert. No matter what the situation is, you should be and are the person best prepared for the weekend. Don't forget. You've seen the schedule. You know where the gaps are. You've seen the curriculum. You know that the craft in the 4-year-old room is going to be messy but kids will love it. Use that knowledge. Lead your volunteers with a confidence that comes from being the right person for the job, and from being well-prepared.

When people walk in, we may have just one chance to give them a reason to come back. God has been preparing them for this day. Maybe they've never been in a church before. Maybe they've been away from church for years. *This* may be the day that Jesus Christ enters their hearts and transforms them into new creations!

We can't let them down. We need to exceed their expectations.

—**Scott**

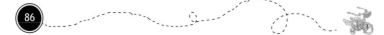

The Number 1 Solution to Your Discipline Challenges

There is one simple word that is the answer to the vast majority of your discipline challenges. The word is *engaged*. When kids are engaged, most discipline challenges quickly fade away.

God made kids to move, to have fun, to participate, to wiggle, to giggle, to laugh, to jump, to play, to talk, to be engaged. If you're having constant discipline challenges, it probably stems from lack of engagement.

So how do you keep kids engaged? How do you grab their attention and hold it? How do you turn chaos into captivation? Here are some proven ways to do just that.

Stay within kids' attention spans. Kids have an attention span of about one minute for every year of age, maxing out at five minutes. That means a 2-year-old has a two-minute attention span, a 4-year-old has a four-minute attention span, and so on.

One of the most successful children's TV programs of all times is *Sesame Street*. The developers of this show knew the secret of staying within children's attention spans. When you stay within children's attention spans, you're well on your way to engaging them. Design your format in segments that last one to five minutes. By creating short segments, you are creating multiple starting and stopping points throughout the time. Every few minutes you're resetting kids' internal attention-span countdown.

Use methods that hold kids' attention. Make sure your communication methods connect with today's kids. There are more ways to share God's Word than just a talking head or a flannel-graph board. You can communicate truth through videos, skits, songs, hands-on activities, games, and more.

Find out what holds the attention of the children in your ministry. Ask them what they enjoy watching, what they enjoy doing. Incorporate their interests in your teaching.

Learn what doesn't engage kids. What causes the kids in your room to disengage? When do you lose their attention? When do they become restless? What is happening when discipline challenges arise? Pinpoint these times, and change or adjust them. We recently noticed that kids grew restless and disengaged when we did announcements with a talking head. We changed it to a video format and saw an immediate improvement in the kids engaging with the announcements.

Set up a camera and film your class time. Go back and watch to see when the kids disengaged. This will help you pinpoint what needs to be adjusted or changed.

Involve kids. To effectively engage kids, you must move beyond just a "good show" that they watch. Kids want to actively participate in the learning process. Involvement equals engagement.

IDEAS

- Let them act out the story, let them hold props—engage them in the learning.

- Use hand motions for the songs you sing. This will draw kids into the worship time and get them more involved.

- Let kids talk. Ask guided questions that will get them talking and discussing the truths you want communicated.

- Use active learning instead of passive listening. Use hands-on activities, crafts, and games.

Engage kids' senses. Multiple sensory learning engages kids. In 1 John 1:1, John talks about his connecting experience with Christ. He says, "We proclaim to you the one who existed from the beginning, whom we have heard and seen. We saw him with our own eyes and touched him with our own hands. He is the Word of life." *Heard. Seen. Touched.* Connecting with Jesus was a sensory experience. Bring taste, touch, sound, sight, and smell as you teach kids about Jesus, and watch them engage.

Check your lessons for sensory learning. Use a minimum of three senses in every lesson. If you want to take engagement to a new level, use all five senses in your lessons.

Engage kids' learning styles. Kids engage in different ways as you tap into their different learning styles. Visual learners engage through seeing. Kinesthetic learners engage through moving, doing, and touching. Auditory learners engage through hearing.

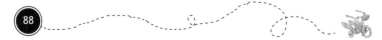

Kids will be engaged in your classroom. The question is, engaged by what? Will it be the truth of God's Word—or with daydreaming, kicking the chairs in front of them, or watching a train going by outside? The time you have to teach kids is too precious to waste. Make sure kids are engaged with truths that will change their lives!

—**Dale**

36

Out of the Box

I've been blessed to lead one of the hardest working, most devoted teams in the world. They are infinitely talented and truly amazing. I love each of them and owe them more than I can ever repay. We've accomplished a lot, made a lot of mistakes, fumbled our way into messes, found our way out of even more, and always kept on going. We've laughed a lot. We've cried a lot. We're a family.

We've also taken our share of field trips. Not often, but from time to time, I tell them to wear their tennis shoes or bring an umbrella " 'cause we're going out." We've gone to lunch, played sports, taken overnight excursions for planning events, ridden go-carts, read books, hit the lake, and done lots of other great things. In these times, we've connected in new ways. In these times, we remember that we're all on the same team for the same reason.

Make some memories. One guy I greatly respect, Craig Jutila, calls this time with his team "Out of the Box." I like that name, and I love to steal ideas from people who've done this longer, or do this better than I do. I must admit, I'm a little jealous of the events Craig manages to arrange. He lives less than an hour from Disneyland, fewer than 30 minutes from the beach, less than two hours from SeaWorld and the San Diego Zoo. Craig lives in Southern California. I live in Oklahoma. I'm close to Frontier City, which is a small amusement park. I'm close to the local zoo. Besides that, we have numerous flat, open fields. Somehow it's just not the same. But wherever you live, you can get creative. Think "Out of the Box!"

If you don't currently plan regular times away with your team, whether paid or volunteer, start today. You'll bless them (and yourself) in ways you never dreamed. They'll get to see you as a human, instead of that person who attends meetings all day and runs past them with your hair on fire. You'll get to have some fun and be one of the team instead of the "leader." You'll learn things, see things, and hear things you never imagined you'd hear coming from these people. Long after all the programs, deadlines, and budgets have faded, you'll remember these times. They're invaluable.

Here are some specific tips.

- Fun doesn't require funds. There are lots of activities you can do that are free or cost very little. Check out your city or county's list of local attractions.

- People love surprises. Well, I do. I don't enjoy getting them, but I enjoy planning them. Make it fun. Don't tell anybody where you're going. Surprise them.

- Make it worth their time. When people lose work time, make sure they don't regret it. By planning events strategically, you can have a great half day (or even whole day) and return refreshed, more productive than before.

You can't survive without your team. Remind them of that often. Even more often, show them. Have fun. Get to know each other. Let the Lord bind your hearts together in love!

—**Scott**

37

Write a Note...Change a Life!

"So encourage each other and build each other up."

—1 Thessalonians 5:11a

Our children's ministry staff meeting is held every Tuesday morning. Part of our time together is spent writing personal notes to some of our volunteer team members. This is a priority for us. We have seen the impact the notes can have. We've had team members come to us with tears in their eyes and thank us. Many times they say it was just what they needed at that time in their lives.

Write notes to your volunteers. Everyone needs to be encouraged. Everyone needs to feel valued. Everyone needs to know he or she is appreciated. A personal note is a great way to accomplish this. Here are some ideas for writing a personal note to a volunteer team member.

IDEAS

- Mention something specific that you saw a volunteer do well. An example would be, "On Sunday I noticed how well you led the activity in your small group. You are doing an awesome job!"

- Let your volunteers know they're making a difference. An example would be, "God is using your service to make a difference in the lives of the kids. Thanks for serving and letting God's love flow through you to them."

- Let volunteers know you care about them as individuals. An example might be, "I count you as a dear friend, and it is a privilege to serve alongside you."

- Pray for the person as you write the note. Say in the note that you prayed.

- Take it to the next level by slipping a gift card in with the note. It doesn't have to be extravagant. Even a $5 gift card can make a person's day.

- Send a quick e-mail every day to a different volunteer. No, not one of those chain e-mails, but a quick, personal e-mail that encourages the person.

Write notes to the kids in your ministry. As adults, we get mail every day, including the 20 credit card applications that arrive. It's no big deal for us. But when a child receives mail, it's a big, big deal. They don't get mail very often. When it does come, it makes them feel important and special. Here are some ideas for writing notes to the kids in your ministry.

IDEAS

- Pray for the kids as you write the notes. Let them know you were thinking of them and praying for them.

- Use the notes to build self-esteem. Let kids know you think they are cool.

- Let kids know you're glad they are part of the ministry.

- Let them know God has a special plan for their lives.

- Keep track of who you have written to so you can make sure to eventually write to every child in your ministry.

- Send birthday cards to the kids in your ministry. Use the cards as an opportunity to show them you care about them and value them. Don't just sign the cards, but take time to write a personal note inside.

One final "note." Use notes to provide a ministry touch when people are hurting. I'll never forget when one of the girls in our ministry lost her father. I wrote her an encouraging note that week. Her mom said God used the note in a great way during that hard time. That was several years ago, and to this day she still has the note.

I have notes as well. They are notes of encouragement and thanks that people have written to me over the years. I keep them in a special place. When I get discouraged, have a bad day, or feel like quitting, I pull out those notes and just start reading. As I read them, the dark clouds drift away and sunshine fills my heart. Many times tears fill my eyes and my burden suddenly grows lighter. As I put the notes away, I am filled with resolve to finish the race God has called me to run.

There is power in your pen. There is life in your pen. There is encouragement in your pen. There is someone who needs the words that can flow out of your pen this week. Go ahead, sit down and do it. Write a note...change a life!

—**Dale**

38

Building a Blockbuster Team

You have to hire. You have to recruit. Whether it's new volunteers or paid staff, it's inevitable. But how do you do it? As you build a team, focus on the whole team. A team is not just the sum of its parts.

Check the four C's.

- Competence. Can this person do what you need him or her to do?

- Character. Does this person have "it"? Will this person work hard, fight through obstacles, and remain true to the objective even when things are difficult?

- Chemistry. Does this person fit your existing team of volunteers and staff? Good rapport often trumps ability.

- Calling. Ask point blank, "Why are you here?" Then listen, really listen, to the answer. Does he or she just need a job? Is the person sacrificing anything to participate in this vision? Is he or she willing to do whatever it takes to be obedient to God's voice, to the call?

What do you already have? What do you need? Well, that all depends. What do you have? Look around. What do you expect out of your team? What jobs or tasks do you still need completed? With the help you currently have, where does that leave you? Refocus each member of your team on his or her individual strengths and yourself on yours. What's left? Where are the gaps? Does the potential team member possess the strengths to fill them? Problem solved.

—Scott

39

The Haunting Detail!

"If you are faithful in little things, you will be faithful in large ones."

—Luke 16:10a

Have you ever had a volunteer walk up and ask about a detail you were supposed to take care of? Your face flushes as you realize you dropped the ball. Have you ever had a parent ask why you didn't return a phone call? Your heart skips a beat as you realize you forgot.

Details may seem small at the time they come along, but when you don't take care of them, they have a way of coming back to haunt you. Children's ministry is made up of lots of little details. The details aren't always glamorous, but they are necessary. It's vital you take care of them. Taking care of details with excellence is what separates great children's ministries from good children's ministries. Here are some simple but effective tips about taking care of the "little things."

Write it down! Write it down! Write it down! When a detail doesn't get taken care of, almost always it's because it wasn't written down. I have been in meetings where an assignment was given and the person didn't write it down. Sure enough, it didn't get taken care of. Discipline yourself to immediately write down assignments when they are given to you.

Carry a blank notecard with you or use a voice recorder during weekend services. If a parent or volunteer asks you to do something, stop and immediately write it down or record a note. On Monday transfer the notes to your to-do list and take care of them.

Return phone calls ASAP. We've all had times when we've left a message for a person or place of business and they didn't return the call. It makes you feel devalued and you wonder why they don't have their act together. When a parent or volunteer leaves a message for you, do your best to return the call within the day. This shows you value the caller and want to help.

Proofread! Proofread! Proofread! One of my pet peeves is typos. Typos are simply small details that got overlooked. And trust me, when they get overlooked by you, other people notice. They may or may not say anything, but it causes them to wonder why you can't take care of details.

Have three people proofread anything you put in print or on screen. It's hard for one person to catch all typos.

Live by lists. Make a list of all the details that need to be done for the upcoming program or event. No matter how small the detail may seem, put it on the list! Keep the list close by, and make sure everything gets done. On game day, you'll be glad you did!

I learned this the hard way. Early in my ministry, I decided to have a cookout for the young couples' class I was teaching. The cookout was way out in the woods. We got to the cookout area and started the fire. I pulled out the hot dog buns and then my heart stopped as I reached down into the bag and realized I had forgotten to get hot dogs. We were at least 30 minutes from the nearest store, and there was no way to get the hot dogs in time. The hungry couples (that I had taken way out in the woods and now couldn't feed) were kind and gracious to me during my embarrassment. But I'm sure they were thinking, "What a goofball!" I know that's what I was thinking. You know why there were no hot dogs? Because there was no list! It was a rude awakening for me to start living by lists!

God has promised to bless and reward those who are faithful in the little things. As you faithfully take care of the little details, you will begin to gain credibility with kids, parents, and members of your team. This credibility will then blossom into confidence. People will know when they ask you to do something, they can consider it done. Over the course of time, your ministry will become known as a ministry of excellence—a ministry not haunted by forgotten details!

—**Dale**

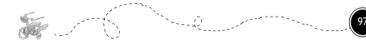

Things change. Get used to it. In modern ministry, if you're not changing (often), it means you're dead. We don't change the message of truth nor the hope of life in Christ…but we do change the delivery. Changing the package, that's where we live. In our ministry, the only constant is change. We try something and fail. Adjust. Try again. Fail. Adjust. Try again. Fail. Repeat. Adjust. Try again. Succeed. We keep that successful way for a while, and then start all over again.

In one recent season of great change, the Lord shared a ruler for our team to use to measure whether we were accomplishing everything we should be. Our leadership team had just clarified the organization's overall vision. An acrostic emerged almost immediately: S-I-M-P-L-I-F-Y.

S is for Stop. Often we're so busy preparing for the upcoming weekend, or doing what we need to do every week, that we forget to stop and listen to God—especially as we contemplate change. But it's essential. Be still. Listen. Stop.

I is for Identify. What needs to change? What is leadership asking of you? What areas require your immediate attention? Track them on a white-board in bright red ink. Be clear. What are we doing? Why are we doing that? Why are doing it *this way?* What needs to change? Identify it.

M is for Measure. How are you doing? In the things you're being asked to do, in the areas you want to change—how's it going? Are you accomplishing what you need to? Is your team firing on all cylinders? Be honest with yourselves. Where do you stand? Watch a clear picture emerge. Measure everything you can.

P is for Purpose. As you identify what you need to change, celebrate it. Get your team behind you. Make it exciting and real. Lead your team in an attitude of doing whatever it takes to make the change. Set a timeline. Set deadlines. Reward completed work.

L is for Learn. Do your homework. Look to others who have already achieved success in the areas you're addressing. Do things right the first time. Don't make mistakes that you could realistically avoid. You don't want people—especially your team—questioning later whether the transition was worth what it cost. Learn what you need to do to be successful.

I is for Innovate. You may have to generate your new plan from scratch. If God calls you to do it, or if leadership asks you to do it, then your creative God will provide the way. Just look at Redbox. Have you seen those things around town? Talk about innovation! It's a simple, straightforward delivery system for DVDs. It's so simple. In your arena, don't overcomplicate. Innovate. What great ideas does the Holy Spirit want to birth through your ministry? Blaze a trail! Go for it!

F is for Focus. Your team needs you to keep them on track. Frankly, that's your job. If you don't do anything else, encourage them, hold them accountable, and demonstrate that you believe in them. Don't let "fires" steal your drive. Keep your mind on the goal, not looking to the right or the left. Press on, straight ahead, until you reach the finish line. Strive for pinpoint accuracy. If you allow even a slight wander, you'll find yourself miles from where you intended to be. Focus.

Y is for You. Stand strong in your calling. You're the leader God appointed to carry out this mission. Accept it. Equip your team. Help them succeed. Clearly identify their roles, and help them understand that without total effort from everyone, the team as a whole can't succeed. Praise them, both privately and in front of their peers. Make every effort to keep the unity of the Spirit through the bond of peace. That's what real synergy is. Together, *you* can do this.

Whether it's finding a new curriculum, planning your first summer camp or VBS, or starting an outreach program—whatever the task, if God has given you the vision, or if your leadership has given you the responsibility, you can do it. Don't overcomplicate it. Don't try to go it alone. Just roll up your sleeves and get to work.

Simplify!

—Scott

41

Putting "Children" in Children's Ministry!

"But Samuel, though he was only a boy, served the Lord."

—1 Samuel 2:18a

There are many accounts in the Bible of kids serving the Lord. Samuel is a great example. He served alongside Eli in the Tabernacle and was used by God, even at an early age.

It is vital that we give children the opportunity to serve. For too long we have made church a spectator sport for kids. We tell them to "sit still and be quiet." And then they grow up and we ask them to volunteer as adults. And guess what they do? They sit still and are quiet.

We must teach kids that it's every Christ-follower's responsibility to serve others. We must raise up a generation of kids who believe that serving is a vital part of following Christ.

There are many ways kids can serve at church. Here are some of the things we're doing to get kids involved.

Kids can serve on the praise team. Kids love to sing, so use that natural affinity to your advantage.

IDEAS

- Have a weekly or monthly rehearsal. Kids must commit to attend this rehearsal to be on the team.
- Make a monthly DVD illustrating song hand motions so they can also practice at home.
- Give them matching shirts. Make the shirts fun and colorful.
- Meet with them before the service and have a time of prayer.
- Rotate the kids so many kids have the opportunity to serve. You can rotate based on your needs and scheduling.

Kids can serve on the greeter team. Kids can play a major role in making new kids feel welcome.

IDEAS

- Have a training session for new greeters.
- Make a name badge for each greeter.

Kids can help in setup and cleanup. We have multiple services with only 20-30 minutes between some of them. Kids play a big part in straightening chairs, picking up paper, and gathering supplies.

IDEAS

- Enlist and train setup and cleanup teams.
- Do you have kids whose parents usually pick them up late? These kids usually love to have a job to do while they're waiting.

Kids can be assistant room directors. Our room directors make sure the small-group leaders have all their activity supplies. Kids can serve as assistants and help distribute and collect supplies.

IDEA

- Do you have kids who attend more than one service? How about letting them attend one service as a participant and serve as a volunteer during the other?

Kids can help with sound and tech. Technology is a way of life for today's kids. In many cases, they can serve in your sound/tech areas just as well as, or even better than, adults.

IDEAS

- Provide hands-on training for kids who want to serve in this area.
- Look for kids who can focus and follow your cues during the service.
- Provide adult supervision for them as needed.

Kids can serve on the drama team. Recently I watched several of our kids do a great job acting in skits. They had practiced their lines and were well-prepared. The kids listened to them carefully, and the real-life situation they acted out drove home this month's teaching truth.

- Have a weekly drama practice to prepare for weekend services. We hold ours on Tuesday night.

- Make the scripts available a minimum of one week before kids will be acting so they have plenty of time to memorize their lines.

- Have an adult leader for them to report to at least 30 minutes before the service. This holds them accountable and lets them go over their lines one last time together.

The kids in your ministry are eagerly awaiting opportunities to serve. Does it take work, training, and supervision to see it happen? Absolutely! Is it worth it? Absolutely!

About a year ago, I noticed a boy standing in the hallway next to his grandmother. She served at one of our check-in kiosks. She told me privately he had no interest in the children's environments. I invited him to come into the room, but to no avail. After a few weeks, I felt led to ask him if he liked computers. Surprise, surprise, he said yes. Long story short, I got him to come in and begin serving on our tech team. God began to work in his life. Even though he wasn't sitting in the audience, he was listening to the lessons as he served in the tech booth. Soon his grandmother was telling me that he was talking about the lessons on the way home. God continued to work. After about a year, he stepped across the line of faith and accepted Christ as his leader and forgiver and friend. He was recently baptized. And it all started by asking him to serve.

There are Samuels in your children's ministry. God is waiting to work in them and through them as they serve. Ask them, train them, encourage them—and watch what God does!

—**Dale**

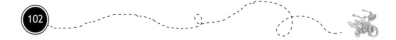

Speak Now or Forever Hold Your Peace

I've been privileged to perform numerous wedding ceremonies. In the old days, we used to say, "Speak now or forever hold your peace." That's true in the ministry role where God, the sovereign creator of the universe, placed you for this season. Are you walking in that confidence?

Speak up or lose out. You're the leader of your ministry. You know best what your ministry needs to succeed. What do you need? More help? Money? Space? Leadership development? A new puppet? A new check-in system? Then say so. Speak up…or forever hold your peace.

If you don't, who will? Who's going to speak for the 2-year-olds? Who will ensure the rooms are safe? It's you. It's your job. It's your privilege.

The Scouts had this right: Always be prepared. There's nothing worse than wasting a chance to speak before church leaders, your pastors, parents, or volunteers. Imagine every opportunity as a presentation to a packed executive board room. Have your material and supporting data ready. Be prepared to defend your position. Dress the part.

Understand your audience. People respond differently. If your senior pastor is a visionary, then hit him with the big stuff. Grab his heart. Don't bore him with spreadsheet details. Speak to him in a language he understands. On the other hand, if you're talking to the finance team, spreadsheet details are what they want. If you're speaking to parents or volunteers, be ready to answer "What does this have to do with me? How will this benefit me or my family?" Know your audience. Prepare accordingly.

Pick your battles. Be selective in what you ask for. Whether your request is granted or denied, document the outcome. Report back to leadership honestly, fully. You're only one of many vying for their time and funds. Don't ask unless you need.

Be patient. As you begin to be more assertive, and as you align more with your pastor and church leadership, your voice will strengthen. You'll earn their respect. Give it time. Stand up and fight for what has to be done today, but patiently and strategically work toward your long-term goals.

God chose you to stand in this role. Your leadership chose you. Show them—and show yourself—that this was absolutely the right decision. Start small, be wise, and speak up.

If you don't, who will?

—**Scott**

Make It Stick!

> "You have been taught the holy Scriptures from childhood, and they have given you the wisdom to receive the salvation that comes by trusting in Christ Jesus."
>
> —2 Timothy 3:15

Today's kids are bombarded with information. A constant deluge of commercials, technology, and media surges toward them. All kids hear becomes a unified noise in their ears, and a single sound is hard to pick up. The kids see a blur, and an individual image can easily become lost.

But the truth of God's Word is the most important message they can ever hear. It is the answer for their lives. We must find ways to raise our message above the noise. How can we make what we teach stick? Here are a few ideas. Translate these principles into your teaching, and it can become "sticky!"

Repeat the point. Decide the essential truths you want to teach kids. Start with the end in mind. What do you want the kids to know, do, and be when they leave your ministry? Turn your essential truths into simple core statements. Let those statements be the foundation of what you teach. (Of course, the statements must be based on biblical truth.) Then repeat, repeat, repeat those simple core statements.

Engage the brain. Research in brain-based learning shows that our brains love to solve mysteries and problems. That's how we're wired. Jesus often taught using parables that made people think, solve, and draw their own conclusions. Secret messages for kids to decode, mysteries to solve—those are the kinds of things that keep kids interested. Incorporate ways to keep kids intrigued, rather than being a "talking head" in the front of the room.

Keep it concrete. Kids, especially younger kids, are concrete thinkers. They process information literally. So use concrete, visual images and objects to portray abstract ideas. We recently used the concrete idea of the cross being a bridge back to God. This image helped them understand what Jesus' death on the cross meant.

Make it memorable. Where were you when you heard what was unfolding on 9/11? Probably everyone can answer that question. Events that have emotion tied to them quickly become entrenched in our long-term memory banks. In *The Dirt on Learning* by Thom and Joani Schultz, the authors say that emotion is the glue of learning and retention.

Create experiences where kids feel emotion. For example, if you're teaching about Noah, dim the lights and play sound effects of thunder, rain, wind, and animal noises. Have kids rock back and forth as if they're in a boat on a stormy sea. Let them feel the emotions Noah must have felt inside the ark. Then ask questions that will open doors to discuss the truth that the emotion is tied to.

One day the kids we're teaching will be faced with temptation and will have decisions to make. In that very moment, may the truth we have taught start ringing in their ears. May the truth be stuck to them so well that they can't shake it off...so well that they make the right choices!

—**Dale**

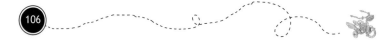

44

Stick a Sign in the Yard

Before ministry, I sold residential real estate for years. I worked in the largest, most successful office in my community. I worked with people who had different sales styles, different work ethics, different personal goals and abilities. Different agents had different theories about how to be successful.

Everything's not up to you…Scripture says every good and perfect gift comes from God. There's always a "God factor" in everything we do. Through his providential hand, he oversees what we do. But we must do our part. Simply sticking a sign in the yard is not enough.

…except the part that's up to you. A mentor once told me, "The harder I work, the more I find myself in the right place at the right time." Did you get that? Does a pro golfer win golf tournaments without bringing his God-given abilities to bear? Does a high-powered CEO sit playing solitaire in his office, hoping for the best? God gives us each unique skills and abilities. We must use them to bring him glory. Understand: *God* brings the increase. But James 2 tells us clearly that faith without accompanying action is "dead."

What has God already told you to do? What's your part? Do it. Is God waiting for you? Act. He'll pour out blessings. What have you been putting off? Do it now. Paint a wall, write an encouraging letter, have the hard talk with your leadership, find a way to pick up kids whose parents won't bring them to your ministry. Do something.

Start small if you have to. But start now. My pastor says, "Everyone ends up somewhere. Few people end up somewhere *on purpose.*" Many times, the smallest actions over time yield the greatest results. Start now. Trust God to bless your efforts, multiply your time, enhance your gifts…and maybe move in a way you never dreamed. Do your part.

—**Scott**

45

Leading Up

A great children's ministry impacts not only kids, but the whole church. A high-impact children's ministry contributes heavily to the overall health and growth of the church. It influences decisions that are made by church leadership. In other words, an effective children's ministry leads up.

Tired of just being considered a "baby-sitting ministry"? Tired of being stuck in a back room somewhere and not getting any "air time" in the big room? Tired of having to beg for enough money just to purchase glue sticks? Tired of not being heard? It's time to start leading up.

Leading up begins by following well. I've had the privilege to serve under some great pastors and leaders in the last 18 years. Each of these people has shaped my life and ministry in a positive way. I learned early on that being a good leader begins by being a good follower.

Loyalty is vital if you're going to lead up. It is an honor to help a pastor and church leadership build a ministry. Let it be known to all that you support the vision and mission of the pastor and church leadership. That doesn't mean that you will always agree with every decision that's made. No one agrees with everyone else all the time. I don't even agree with myself half the time. But what it does mean is that once a decision is made, you stand behind the pastor and church leadership...and everyone knows it.

Disgruntled members know if they try to complain to you about the pastor or church leadership, they will not find a welcome ear. It means when you have a complaint, you take it up to the leadership above you...not sideways to those around you or to those under your leadership.

As the pastor and leadership see that you are committed to the overall vision of the church and not just to "building your kingdom," they will welcome your influence.

Lead up with fruit. Ask God to produce fruit through your life and ministry. You want to get the attention of your pastor? Start reaching families. Lead your ministry to grow. Nothing speaks louder than fruit. As the leadership of the church sees your ministry growing and lives being changed, you can be sure you will have their ears. A children's ministry that is a growth engine for the church will have a place at the leadership table.

Lead up with vision. Having a vision for the children's ministry is essential if you're going to lead up. Know where you're headed. Look into the future and see what can be. Dream big. Share the vision with leadership. As they see your passion and hear your visionary thinking, they will buy into what God has placed in your heart.

Lead up by championing the importance of children's ministry. Keep the value of children's ministry in front of church leadership. Pass along articles, statistics, e-mails, and books that show how important children's ministry is to the health and growth of the church. That doesn't mean you constantly bombard them or become annoying. It simply means you occasionally pass these things along when there is an open door.

Lead up by open communication. Keep your pastor and leadership informed of what is going on in your ministry. Share reality, but don't whine. Need more space? Show them why. Need more money? Have a plan to show how you are going to use it. Need more staff? Have detailed job descriptions and proof of why you need to hire additional staff. Schedule a lunch appointment occasionally with the pastor or leadership, and communicate to them what's happening in the children's ministry. A lunch appointment is a better way to communicate than stopping them in the hallway before a weekend service.

Take the necessary steps to start leading up and you'll see children's ministry becoming a major catalyst for your church. Your pastor and church leaders want to see it happen. They're just waiting for you to start leading up!

—**Dale**

Day two of VBX (that's VBS). Kids are everywhere. It's my first year in ministry, and our biggest summer event yet. I'm trying to keep my head above water and make sure no one gets hurt.

Even with our summer event still in full swing, we had to start planning for our fall discipleship program. I had just hired a new team member, Kendra, to help lead that discipleship program, the same program we'd been using for the last few years. Kendra made a routine phone call to the author to ask for the curriculum guides. The voice on the other end informed her that they were in the process of revising the curriculum...and they weren't going to be able to make it available to us. But we were supposed to start in three weeks! With that one phone call, I felt everything come to a screeching halt. I hung my head in disbelief, imagining a huge red sign in front of me:

STOP.

Have you ever been there? You've just started to gain some momentum, and bam! You're smacked in the face with a STOP sign? Have you ever felt like you're just starting to get the hang of this gig when suddenly you're reminded how incompetent you are? Have you ever sat, stuck at the intersection, staring at your STOP sign, feeling like you want to cry? I feel your pain.

Think about what "everything" means. We all face roadblocks. Those seemingly insurmountable hurdles that stop us cold. In times like those, we must remember the truth of God's Word:

"And we know that God causes everything to work together for the good of those who love God and are called according to his purpose for them" (Romans 8:28).

The Bible says "everything." God promises to use everything for our good. Amazing! Why is it so easy to forget that promise?

Because we're hurting, and the pain is real.

Because when the storm is raging, it's hard to see the truth.

Because change is difficult.

Because we're human.

Pull out all the STOPs. I've learned that what seems to be a STOP sign more often is actually a YIELD. Usually it's placed there for my protection. Other times it's actually a DETOUR. In those times, God's preparing us for greater impact. When you feel like you just got kicked in the gut and all you can see in front of you is STOP, look again. Remember Romans 8:28. Look closer. Maybe it's not a STOP sign at all.

Review your options. Kendra and I each took a deep breath. Even though we were exhausted and emotionally drained by the bad news we'd just received, we closed ranks and started talking. Starting from square one always seems like such a daunting challenge. But then you realize what that really means: We can go anywhere from here.

Pray and ask: Right turn? Left turn? Straight ahead? I explained to the team what we had just found out and that now we needed God to tell us what to do instead. I remember feeling so overwhelmed. Then we prayed as a team. We asked God to reveal his plan and to help us be obedient. We considered just buying something and throwing it in at the last minute, but we never felt like that's what he wanted. Instead, I began to share what God had placed in my heart, and Kendra began to describe and shape what she thought that might look like.

Commit, turn the wheel, and press the accelerator to the floor. We took the detour, pressed our noses firmly against the grindstone...and made it happen. Three weeks later, KONNECT began.

That was three years ago. The program we started throwing together in last-minute desperation, born out of need, driven by passion, and shaped with vision, has since evolved into the greatest example of who we are and who we desire to be. KONNECT has more LifeKIDS' DNA in it than anything else we do. Families have been changed. *We've* been changed.

Here's the funny thing in this story. God never lost his cool. Not once. He was working for our good. He was carrying out his will. There wasn't really a STOP sign, like we thought. Instead, it was a DETOUR, an opportunity to do something we may have never done otherwise.

What's ahead on your road?

—**Scott**

Welcome Aboard!

Imagine being grabbed from your adult Bible study class, propelled down the hall, and forced toward an open doorway. Nearing the room, you see dozens of out-of-control kids running around. Their high-pitched wails pierce your ears. A lady sits in a chair in the corner, a desperate look in her glazed eyes. Her hand trembles as she holds out a teachers book and whispers, "Thank God you're here!"

The above scenario is an obvious exaggeration, but it's a small picture of what new volunteers feel like when you don't bring them on the team properly. It's vital that you have a process in place to introduce new volunteers to your ministry. Here is the process that we follow.

Interest card. Anyone expressing an interest in serving is asked to fill out an interest card. It's a simple card that gives us basic contact information and lets the person indicate which age level he or she would like to serve.

Observation. Next we invite prospective volunteers to come and observe the environment in action. The key word at this point is *observe*—not *serve*. Introduce them to key team members while they are in the environment. Ask team members to share the blessings they get out of serving. Before the session begins, spend a few minutes giving an overview of the environment. Experiencing the environment can help people decide if this is the place for them.

One-on-one interview. Take time in the interview to get to know the person, and help determine if the person's schedule and gifts are good fits for your ministry. See Idea 65 for more details on what to cover in this interview.

Serving application. If there are no red flags, give the prospective volunteer a serving application to fill out. This is a thorough questionnaire and background-check form.

Background check and reference calls. It is critical that you do a background check and make at least two reference calls for anyone who is going to serve in your ministry. This is non-negotiable. (Background checks can be done through churchvolunteercentral.com and others.)

Orientation. Once the background check and reference calls are clear, we invite each volunteer to an orientation. We provide at least one orientation every month. The orientation should be well-prepared and done with excellence. This will show potential team members that you highly value them and that they are going to be part of a first-class ministry. Use the orientation to give an overview of the ministry, share core values and mission statements, and cover essential components such as safety and security, policies, and procedures.

Ongoing training. Hands-on training is a must. Match new volunteers with seasoned team members who can mentor them. The time frame for this depends on the position and the new team member's experience. Make some of your training available online. We have online training videos that we require each new team member to watch. Then do a follow-up interview two to four weeks after they have started serving.

How you bring on new team members will set the standard for their entire time of serving. When you say "Welcome aboard," make sure it's done with excellence!

—**Dale**

Have you ever planned an evening with friends? It always comes up: "Where do we want to eat?" Inevitably, at least with our friends, this one simple question launches a half-hour discussion: "Oh, I don't care." "Wherever you want." "Anything but Thai." It's difficult to navigate such discussions. And this is just dinner!

When it comes to making decisions about your children's ministry, you have to be intentional.

Ask the tough questions. When I first started in ministry, our church had gone more than six months without a children's pastor. Leadership had decided they wouldn't hire anyone until they knew they had "the right person." As it happened, they decided that was me.

When I came into the ministry, I joined a team of six ladies already in place. I distinctly remember my first day, not only because of the purple office I inherited, but also because of the difficult conversations we had that day. I scheduled 30 to 45 minutes with each team member.

I started each session with some small talk, to sort of break the ice. After things were rolling, I looked each person in the eye and asked with conviction, "Are you called to this ministry?" About half were caught off guard, and the other half never missed a beat. As each person prepared her answer, I analyzed her body language, her expressions, and how she handled herself in a difficult conversation, all of which would be skills crucial to our future success as team.

This matters. God's calling is perhaps the most important asset we have to be successful in ministry. You can delegate tasks, and you can borrow creativity or build it up over time. But when everything else is going wrong, you have to know you're where you are because God called you to be there.

One answered, "I really have no idea." Another said, "I absolutely know that I'm called to ministry, just not necessarily to children." Others said they knew without a doubt that they were exactly where God wanted them. When they responded this way, I followed up with, "How do you know that?" Their answers varied, but I heard things such as "What I do completes something in me" and "The feeling I get when I realize that we're part of the bigger picture of what God is doing is like nothing else in the world." Another said something like, "I know because on days when I don't want to do it anymore, when I'm tired or someone's mad, when I'm at the end of my rope, God reminds me that this is *his* call, it's *his* ministry, and that it's what I was created to do."

Lead. Remember the dinner conversation? People need someone to take charge, to lead. Make decisions with confidence and resolve. Lead with the confidence that God has called you to where you are and that he's fully equipping you for his purposes. Tell yourself:

I am a leader, called by God, to carry out his purpose in this time and place. As such I will:

- make decisions for my team with confidence and resolve;
- act quickly when action is needed;
- remain under the authority of the Word of God, the Holy Spirit, and my church leadership;
- admit when I am wrong;
- celebrate when we are successful; and
- trust God for this calling upon my life.

Six years later, three of the original six team members are still with the church. They have become some of my dearest friends. They're my most trusted allies. They're amazing women, called by God, who exemplify that calling by providing excellence in all they do for his name and his kingdom.

—**Scott**

Ahhhh…summertime. For most people it means a long vacation, relaxation, and more personal time. Not if you're a children's pastor! Summer can be one of the busiest, most intense times of the year.

Here are five tips for how to not only survive, but thrive, during the summer months.

Have a "Summer Serve" program. Summer usually finds children's ministries scrambling for volunteers. Regular volunteers take time off or go on vacation. And that's good. Your volunteers need to rest; they need to take time to be refreshed. Encourage them to do so. But it can leave you with volunteer holes to fill. Create a sign-up sheet that lists all the weekends. Then ask parents to sign up for one or more weekends. Most parents are glad to help out at least one weekend. You will also find that many of them stick around and become regular volunteers.

Consider doing less. Many children's ministries fill their summer calendars with trips, events, vacation Bible school, and camp. As a result, they end up doing a lot of things with mediocrity. Consider trimming back some of those calendar dates and just doing a few things extremely well. Decide how you can have the biggest impact, and focus on that.

For us, our biggest impact happens in our weekend services. That is where we bear the most fruit—even during the summer. We guard the time, energy, and resources that go into the weekend services, even during the summer. We do an early-elementary sleepover and an upper-elementary camp, and that's it for the summer. This allows us to keep our focus on the weekend services.

Do a fun summer teaching series. Make your summer teaching series fun, fun, fun! Instead of checking out for the summer and just coasting along, plan a fun, relevant series that kids can connect to. Give them fresh bread from God's oven instead of reheated leftovers. Effectively engage kids with God's Word in the summer, and you can see your attendance maintain or even grow!

Plan your vacation to fit the flow. You need vacation time and rest, just like everyone else. Find the best time during the ministry year to take your time off. It might not be summer. I have made the mistake before of taking a vacation a few weeks before a big summer event. I paid for it when I got back. Now I take my vacations outside of summer when possible. If you do take a summer vacation, make sure you have plenty of time to take care of business before you leave and after you get back. You want to enjoy your vacation instead of stressing about how you're going to pull off everything when you get back.

Adjust your weekend programming as needed. Summer is a great time to do some big rallies with all the kids together. Perhaps bring in special guests. During the summer months, we adjust and don't have small groups. We go with a longer large-group time and a short activity time. This gives our small-group leaders the opportunity to take time off if they want. It also gives the kids a change for a few months.

The tough thing about summer is you finish up, and wham!—the fall season is right in your face! Fall is normally a time of growth. You don't want to go into fall limping from the crazy days of summer. So try some of the tips above. They'll help you enter the fall season feeling strong instead of in a summer daze!

—**Dale**

He made millions in real estate. Lost it all. Then made it back again. According to Wikipedia, he's on his third marriage. He's one of the largest American holders of commercial real estate. He's an acclaimed public speaker and a best-selling author. Even with all these "accomplishments," what's he known for? Bad hair and "You're fired!"

The Donald. Mr. Trump. The man, the legend. Regardless of what you think of him, you have to admire his drive, his entrepreneurial spirit, his success. If you're a real estate–shark wannabe, he's the one to watch. (Conveniently, here in America, all you have to do is turn on the TV!)

You may not think The Donald possesses a single quality you'd want to emulate. Maybe. But watching just one episode of *The Apprentice* could teach you how to radically improve your ministry. You can learn how to look a person straight in the eye and say, "You're fired."

It's an ugly job, but guess what? You're the one who has to do it.

Acknowledge the good...*and* the bad. Over the years, we've learned that not everyone is "a fit" for our children's ministry. They're not bad people—they passed the mandatory background check, after all. They're simply not working out, and they're not going to change. At times, this means releasing someone from your ministry.

It won't be easy. You're not likely to see their past behavior suddenly transform into a wonderful, gracious attitude when you share your decision. But it's the right thing to do. In 1 Corinthians, Paul warns us to not be misled: Bad company corrupts good character. Most people refer to this passage when they're talking about friendships, about the company we keep. But truth is truth. This principle applies just as much to your ministry as anywhere else. The wrong people can (and will) become a cancer that eats at your ministry from within, sometimes doing harm that's beyond your repair.

Pray. Pray for the individual and about the situation. Constant, effective prayer yields tangible results. Often the Holy Spirit intervenes on your behalf. Other times, he may change your outlook toward the difficult volunteer(s).

Talk face to face, directly to the individual. You may want to avoid direct conflict. Often it "feels" better to share "challenges and opportunities" with your entire group, hoping that the one or two individuals will "get it." They probably won't. The conscientious servants ask themselves, "What have I done wrong?" And your intended audience thinks, "What have they done wrong?" Meet with the person in question face to face (with another ministry representative present), and address the issues head-on.

Clearly identify the issue(s), and be direct about the solution(s). "You've arrived late three of the last four weeks. This isn't fair to the others you serve with, and it makes it difficult for us to begin on time. I need you to commit to arrive ____ minutes before the service begins" (whatever your policy is). Then hold the person accountable.

Create consequences. Real life has consequences. If you floss, you keep your teeth longer. If you don't pay your electric bill, they turn off your lights. People need clear expectations. They need to understand that you *will* make changes if things don't improve. Let them know clearly what will happen. Then follow through.

Protect even difficult volunteers in front of others. It's so easy to "share" your frustrations or problems with other volunteers. It's a fine line between gossip and "Would you pray for me for ____?" Unless the person you're talking to is part of the solution, sharing goes beyond bad manners—directly into sin. We're clearly instructed to steer clear of gossip and slander. And if you hear it from others, put a stop to it immediately.

Consider positive options. Would this person "fit" better in an alternate role? Maybe he or she could do data entry for you on a home computer. Many times a simple role change can not only remedy a negative situation, but even allow the person to use his or her gifts in a positive way.

Never burn a bridge. Have you ever been wrong about anything? Me, too. Many times God uses situations like these to change a person's heart. Make restoration your goal wherever possible.

Trust God. Sometimes it may seem like having somebody—anybody— is better than having no one. Not true. God will provide the resources you need as you cast your vision and grow your ministry. In situations where moral failure, inappropriate behavior, or angry outbursts clearly endanger your children or your ministry, remove the person immediately, and involve leadership as quickly as possible. In less serious situations, where it's negativity, personality conflicts, habitual tardiness, a lack of focus, or other subjective circumstances, use your discernment. That's why you have it.

—**Scott**

51

Don't Be a Bubble Boy!

"The Son of Man, on the other hand, feasts and drinks, and you say, 'He's a glutton and a drunkard, and a friend of tax collectors and other sinners!' "

—Luke 7:34

Some Christ-followers pull away from the current culture and place themselves inside a "Christian bubble." They think the more you are out of touch with the culture, the more godly you are. They might pop out of the bubble occasionally to quote a Bible verse to someone on the outside, but they hastily retreat back inside.

Jesus definitely wasn't in the bubble. The Bible says he ate with "tax collectors and other sinners." He didn't pull away from those who needed God's truth the most. Rather, he hung out with them. He ate with them. He went to their homes. He got involved in their lives. He was right in the middle of the culture of his day. The "religious" people didn't like it. You could hear their shouts coming from inside the bubble as they called him "the friend of sinners." What a great thing to be called!

We are called to reach the culture in which we live. We must meet people where they are. But it's hard to build relationships outside the bubble…if you're never outside of the bubble. If you don't know about people's music, entertainment, styles, and tastes, then it will be hard to connect with them. They will look at you as you sit inside the bubble, and say, "That's weird. I want no part of that."

The same principle applies to children's ministry. We have to get outside our little "bubble" songs, "bubble" DVDs, and "bubble" books, and know the culture that kids live in today. As I stated in another chapter, missionaries spend lots of time learning the culture of the people they are trying to reach. We are missionaries to children. We must know what's going on in their culture. We have to speak their cultural language if we want them to listen to us.

So how do you get outside the bubble and connect with kid culture? Here are some ways to burst out of the bubble.

Read magazines. Here are some key magazines that will keep you in touch with kid culture.

- American Girl
- Kidscreen (a must-have—order from kidscreen.com)
- Sports Illustrated Kids
- Boys' Life
- Discovery Girls
- Girls' Life
- Children's Ministry Magazine (especially the "Keeping Current With Kids" section)

Regularly check out children's TV programming. Here are the big four to watch.

- Disney Channel
- Nickelodeon
- Cartoon Network
- MTV (for preteens—like it or not, a lot watch it)

Watch movies kids like. Find out what kids are watching at the box office and on DVD. Ask kids on a regular basis what their favorite movies are. Then take time to watch them. You can also check out fandango.com or pluggedin.com to see what's currently playing and get reviews.

Know what video games kids are playing. Ask kids to tell you about their favorite games and why they like them. Go by the video game store and ask the sales clerk what the most popular games are for kids. Read reviews about the games. Rent the games and check them out if you have a game system.

Know their music. Music is a great reflection of culture. Ask kids what's on their iPod. See what's at the top of the Billboard charts. Ask kids who their favorite singers are.

Know their favorite websites. Ask kids where they spend time on the Web, then check out the sites. Find out what Internet game sites they frequent.

Go to websites that give insight into kid culture. Here are a few I like to check out:

- kidscreen.com
- connectwithkids.com
- nick.com
- familyeducation.com

Want more? Just Google "kid culture" to find more information.

Regularly walk through the toy aisles. Look at the newest toys. Keep abreast of what kids are clamoring for.

Have kids' focus groups. Talk with groups of kids and ask what's cool right now. Make the group as diverse as possible to get the best answers.

Instead of avoiding the culture, look at it as something that can help you connect kids to Jesus. Be a student of kid culture, and use it as a vehicle to reach out to them.

And when culture collides with God's truth, use it as an opportunity to show what God's Word says about the subject. We want kids to be out in the culture when they grow up so they can reach people.

So if you're in the Christian bubble, burst out! Get out there and learn all you can about kid culture. That's where Jesus wants you...outside the bubble!

—**Dale**

52

The Dream

The scene was surreal, like a theatrical production. I approached the double doors surrounded by a soft haze, like from a smoke machine. They opened automatically. I walked in and stood facing a wall covered floor to ceiling with an elaborate mural. In text decorated like a medieval manuscript, it read:

"Children are a gift from the Lord; they are a reward from him. Children born to a young man are like arrows in a warrior's hands. How joyful is the man whose quiver is full of them!"

I looked up that passage later. It's Psalm127:3-5a. It's strange; I can't remember details of the mural today except for the words—and that I was overwhelmed by its extravagant beauty.

More than bread. After taking it in, I passed through a hallway into a room full of tables with built-in seating, laid out with trays and cups like you might find in an elementary school lunchroom. I looked above the serving window, where yet another large, elaborate mural read:

"Jesus answered, 'It is written: "Man does not live on bread alone, but on every word that comes from the mouth of God." ' "

I later looked this up, too. It's from Matthew 4:4 (NIV).

As much as I've tried since, I cannot remember a single color of that mural, but I vividly remember encountering the beauty of the Word of God, and that there was a sense that its presence in this place carried profound significance.

Working for the Lord. I left the "lunch" room, following the haze drawn throughout the building, passing through rooms with similar settings, each room highlighting a passage from God's Word beautifully emblazed as its focal point. I paused in awe in each room, turning completely around each time, trying to drink everything in. Each area was experiential, not educational. Environmental, not sterile.

One area was clearly designed for activity and to inspire creativity. Its mural read:

"Whatever you do, work at it with all your heart, as working for the Lord, not for men."

This is Colossians 3:23 (NIV).

Children, obey your parents. Each room had a sort of flow, leading me through to the next. As I left one room, I realized it was the last, that I had been traveling in a sort of large arc or circle, and I found myself once again at the first double door, where I had entered. This time, though, the first mural was at my back, and I was facing one last artistic marvel. Its artwork framed the doorway, with the text boldly presented above it. This "exit mural" read:

"Children, obey your parents in the Lord, for this is right."

That's Ephesians 6:1 (NIV).

Again I stood, awestruck, taking it all in. I reread the passage. The doors opened before me. I stepped across the threshold and returned outside as the doors drifted gently closed behind me.

A solemn awakening. I sat up in bed, fully awake. I blinked in the darkness, like my eyes were adjusting from being in the light. I was amazed. Frightened. Intrigued. I looked around. Yup, I was in my own bed, not standing outside, as I had supposed. My wife lay deeply sleeping beside me. It was still dark outside. It was a dream. But not *just* a dream. I lay back and closed my eyes. I began replaying the dream's story in my mind's eye. What did it all mean?

Little did I know that once the Lord had given me this simple, beautiful dream, it would become a focal point of my ministry. Not in its literal interpretation, but in what it represents: what I was supposed to do. I pray the Lord reveals your purpose to you, your vision.

—**Scott**

The Man Factor!

"I searched for a man among them who would build up the wall and stand in the gap before Me for the land, so that I would not destroy it; but I found no one."

—Ezekiel 22:30 (NASB)

Stop for a moment and consider these statistics:

- The church population as a whole is made up of 61 percent women and 39 percent men.

- On any given Sunday there are 13 million more adult women than men in America's churches.

- Twenty-five percent of married churchgoing women attend church alone.

I have found these statistics to be true. As I speak at children's ministry conferences across the country, normally the women in the audience far outnumber the men. It's time we challenge more men to step up and get involved in children's ministry!

Take a look next weekend in your children's ministry environments. Are there men serving? Are there men making a difference?

We have a great team of men who serve in our children's ministry. But guess what? We need a lot more. And I have a hunch that you do, too. How can we see more men enter the spiritual battle for a generation of kids? Here are some things you can do that we are doing to involve more men in children's ministry.

Intentionally enlist men to serve in your children's ministry. Go after them and share the vision of the impact they can make. If your church has a men's ministry, then partner with them to enlist men to serve.

Ask men to lead your boys groups and classes. There is a vast need for boys to have good men as mentors and leaders. Boys need to be in the presence of men. Many boys come from fatherless homes and need positive male role models.

Have men coach and shepherd men. Let men train and mentor other men in your children's ministry. Build a community of men who serve together and challenge each other to grow.

Make sure your ministry has a masculine side. Many times children's ministries are designed to appeal more to women serving. This is reflected in everything from table decorations at training meetings to appreciation gifts. Remember to appeal to men if you want them involved. Most men don't want a "tote bag" to carry their lesson supplies in.

Troy Smith, quarterback from Ohio State, won the Heisman Trophy in 2006 and went on to play in the NFL for the Baltimore Ravens. Troy grew up in a rough neighborhood in Cleveland. As a 9-year-old-boy, he had no father figure in his life. He was being raised by a single mom who at the time had a drug problem.

Across the street from Troy's house was a neighborhood football field. He often wandered over to watch the kids football team practice. Day after day he would come back and watch from the edge of the field. The coach, Irvin White, noticed him one day and asked if he wanted to join the team. Troy said yes and so Coach Irvin went with him to ask his mom's permission. The coach persuaded Troy's mom to let him join the team.

One day after practice, Troy began to cry. Coach Irvin found out that Troy's mother had been sent to jail for drug abuse and Troy had nowhere to turn. Coach Irvin stepped in and fostered Troy. He became the father figure that Troy so desperately needed. He poured his life into Troy and taught him how to be a man. And the rest is history.

This weekend there may be some little Troy Smiths who walk in the door of your church. They will be in desperate need of a man to step into their lives and guide them. What a great opportunity we have to connect them with men who can make a difference in their lives.

—**Dale**

I was driving down the road one day when out of the corner of my eye I saw a big salmon-colored something languishing in a field with a "For Sale" sign slapped on it. I'm naturally curious (and always looking for unusual deals), so I pulled over to check it out. It was an old fire engine. It was pretty beaten up. It had obviously been many years since this machine had seen a fire. I called and asked some questions and learned that it was a 1954 Ford, a *genuine* fire engine.

Rusted a little…and faded *a lot*—I could only imagine its glory days. The owner had purchased it online, planning to use it to water his fields. But when it arrived and he fired it up, he discovered that the tanks were rusted and the pumps "had issues." You wouldn't know it by looking, but he said it actually ran very well. He promised that the engine was strong, the suspension was tight, and the brakes were good. He may have been exaggerating a little, but it *did* run.

Identify (and locate) the resources you need. I asked my boss if we could buy it. He went to look at it with me, and he actually even drove it. Then he asked me the tough question: "How exactly do you propose we pay for this, Scott?" It wasn't much, but money's money, and I didn't have a "Fire Engine" line item in my budget. (I double-checked.) To our excitement, not long after that, God provided the money—almost to the penny—not only for the purchase, but even for its extreme makeover! A guy I knew at our church, Mike, owned a successful auto repair and paint shop. Mike does great work, and he agreed to help us bring our fire engine to life.

Remember who this is for. (Hint: Jesus and the kids.) Now all we needed was a plan. I began dreaming about all the different ways we could use our truck, picturing it as a celebrity in all sorts of scenes. Our hometown has a big Fourth of July parade every year, and we always participate. Several high schools in our area periodically host parades. We would use it for grand openings at new campuses. It would be a huge hit at camp.

I also tried to picture what the kids might like it to look like, and the dream began to take shape in my mind. I decided to paint it solid metallic black, with flames engulfing the front that would lick down the sides, reaching toward the back. I also wanted our logo prominently displayed on both sides and on the back. I was getting more and more excited. This was going to be the coolest thing these kids had ever seen.

Brace yourself for (the inevitable) opposition. Then I told my team. Guess what? For the most part, they...*hated* it! One person said, "It has to be red, Scott...because it's a *fire engine!*" Point taken. Another thought flames were terribly inappropriate for children. She (very passionately) told me, "You might as well call it the *Hellmobile!*" She shouldn't have said that because it made me think, "That's a fantastic idea! Here comes the Hellmobile, crashing through the gates of hell, leading children to the light!"

I stuck to my guns. Do 8-year-olds really care about "authentically" restoring a 1954 fire engine? They don't even know what a 1954 fire engine is! I was certain, however, that they *would* love a huge flaming truck blazing down the street. I got leadership to approve my plan, and we were all set.

Execute. Make it happen. When I shared my vision with Mike, he took it to a whole different level. The result he achieved is simply amazing. It's a beautiful sight to behold! We won first place in the Fourth of July parade that year. Today, our fire engine is an icon, a celebrity personality, just as I had imagined. It's known throughout our community as a representation of our children's ministry, a continuation of our brand. And by the way, once my team actually saw the finished result, they ended up loving it...almost as much as the kids do.

Use it. Reap the benefits of the hard work you've sown. Our truck thunders down the street, blaring Audio Adrenaline's "Big House" or Planet Shakers' "Shake the Planet," with a couple hundred kids streaming along behind, singing at the top of their lungs, doing the hand motions that we choreographed. People see that we're different. It's obvious to them that we're having fun. Most important, they see us glorifying God, lifting up Christ—and they see that we're not afraid to proclaim it in the streets where we live.

What defines your ministry? What makes your ministry stand out? Do you have a logo? Do you have even just one thing that sets you apart from the crowd? If not...*why not?*

Look for ways to brand your ministry. Look for ways to plant that seed in people's minds. Make sure that the image you project expresses both who you really are and what you desire to become. "But my leadership would never allow me to buy something like that!" Really? Have you asked? Have you asked God to provide the funds, the work, the fill-in-your-blank that you'd need? Jesus said we don't have because we don't ask. Maybe it's a hot-air balloon, a great sign outside your building, a fun T-shirt that your kids will wear to school, a cool license plate that your families can display on their cars…you're really only limited by your own imagination and by what you're willing to pursue.

It might even be a 1954 firetruck that someone else called the Hellmobile.

—**Scott**

Huddle Up!

A great football team knows the importance of the huddle. When the team huddles up, it's coming together to show unity, share the action plan, and reconfirm everyone's assignment. Encouragement, inspiration, and strength are found in the huddle.

A great children's ministry team knows the importance of huddling, too. Here are some things that need to happen inside a children's ministry huddle.

Fellowship. Give team members time to hang out and deepen their relationships. This can happen at the beginning of a team meeting. Have icebreaker activities and questions available at the tables. Also, walk around and personally connect with each leader during this time. A pat on the back, a thank you, a smile...they won't forget it!

Celebration. Pause to celebrate victories that have happened since the last team meeting. Give team members time to share stories of successes and blessings they have experienced. Sharing growth numbers is good, but sharing real-life stories of changed lives is even better. We often show video testimonies of kids who have recently been baptized.

Encouragement. Encourage the team. Brag on them. Show them how they are making a difference in the lives of kids. Read positive letters and e-mails from kids and parents to encourage the team.

Highlight a few team members each time you meet. Bring them up and point out specific details of the great job they're doing. Present them with a gift if you choose.

Training. People want to grow and learn. Provide them with quality training in their ministry area. Help them walk away better at what they do.

Challenge. Cast vision for the future. Describe the next level, and challenge them to take the ministry there.

Inspiration. Tug at their heartstrings. Present them with a small gift or keepsake. Inspire them to keep going. Look around during this time—you should see some tears being wiped away.

Prayer. Include time for prayer in small groups and corporately. Pray for both personal and ministry needs. Have prayer cards available at your meetings for team members to write prayer requests. Take time to pray for these requests during the week. Send notes or e-mails letting people know you prayed for their needs.

Plan your team meetings for a time you can get the most members there. Meeting once a quarter works best for us. We meet with individuals or smaller groups of leaders as needed, but the big team meetings are held once a quarter on a weeknight.

I have attended and...I must confess...led some team meetings in the past that were a flop. I've also attended and led some team meetings where we all left pumped up. When you call for a huddle, be well-prepared and ready to lead. Make sure team members leave the huddle encouraged, equipped, and energized!

—**Dale**

56

Serve With Passion

My favorite movie is Mel Gibson's *The Passion of the Christ.* I'm a visual person. Sure, I've read the account of my Savior's sufferings. I've worshipped in gratitude for his incomparable gift. And yet, seeing this film changed my life. I had never *seen* the depth of his love for me, his unwavering determination to fulfill his Father's will. *Seeing* it both changed my life and transformed my ministry.

Jesus knew his time was short. He knew his responsibility. He knew the cost didn't matter. He knew what *had to be done.* What would our ministries look like if our personal mission statements matched his? We must follow Christ's example as we carry on his ministry.

If you can do it today, do it today. Jesus never procrastinated. Often we put things off for later only to find our "later" consumed with issues, problems, or emergencies that we never saw coming.

You're stronger if you have help. Accomplish more by empowering others. Find people you can lead. Ask God for people who will stand beside you, people who "get it." Then welcome them when God answers.

Raise the bar. Where performance is measured, performance improves. People want to be a part of something bigger than they could do on their own. Challenge them, and watch them exceed your expectations.

Extend yourself. Do what you do best. Lead, inspire, cheer. God has equipped you with this ministry. Infuse your passion into others. Live it and breathe it!

Also, make sure your ministry can continue when you're gone. Nobody wants to think about it, but leadership is only for a season. Make sure your team can carry on in your absence.

Submit your will to God's will. Focus on the prize. Don't get caught up in the institution. None of this is about us. Jesus took every opportunity to submit to his Father's will in place of his own. Follow his example. Ask God daily, "Father, where will we go today? What will you have me do today to glorify you and fulfill your plan?"

Set your passion free...through radical obedience. Some days you're going to be tired, beaten up, misunderstood, lied about, maybe even downright despised. Don't give up. Jesus knows your heart. He hears. His Holy Spirit inside you feels your pain. Consistently live obediently and no outsider will be able to deny your calling.

Embrace our Savior's example. Embrace your opportunity. Maximize the impact of the influence you've been entrusted with. Live a life of passion, one worthy of your calling.

—**Scott**

57

It's About the Heart...
Not Just the Head!

"I have hidden your word in my heart, that I might not sin against you."

—Psalm 119:11

We often see the stats about the percentage of kids who walk away from church when they graduate from high school. The percentage varies from report to report, but the fact is that many kids do walk away from church when they graduate.

I believe one major reason is that they have been taught head knowledge without the truth being embedded in their hearts. Head knowledge without heart transformation leads kids to spiritual emptiness.

We must move beyond just filling kids' heads with Bible "facts" to teaching them to follow God from their hearts. Jesus said in Matthew 22:37, "You must love the Lord your God with all your heart, all your soul, and all your mind." Notice what comes first...the heart. Get the heart right, and everything else will follow.

So how do we move kids beyond head knowledge to becoming heart followers of Christ?

Teach kids that becoming a follower of Christ is a heart decision, not just a head decision. Following Jesus is not just a child repeating facts he has been told. It is a child believing in Jesus from the heart. It is a child asking Jesus to be leader...forgiver...friend. We must teach kids that following Jesus is about knowing Jesus, not just knowing *about* Jesus.

IDEAS

- Have a new believers class. Require parents to attend the class with their kids. Explain thoroughly what it means to become a follower of Christ.

- Talk with each child and his or her parents. Make sure the child has a clear understanding of what it means to follow Christ.

Explain Scripture verses. I once used a popular Scripture memory program in a children's ministry I led. We asked kids to quickly memorize dozens of verses. The program tended to be legalistic, and I began to wonder if it was effective. Over time, I saw that it was temporarily filling kids' heads with verses, but the kids had no clue what many of the verses meant or how to apply them.

It caused me to refocus how I teach kids to memorize Scripture. Now I only ask kids to memorize one verse a month. We spend the whole month going over that verse…making sure kids know it thoroughly…explaining what it means…showing kids how to live it out. And the impact has been remarkable. I believe it is better for children to thoroughly learn one verse a month than to quickly place multiple verses in their short-term memory with little or no application.

Always teach application. If you study the teaching style of Jesus, you will see the vast majority of his teaching was application of truth. We tend to do the opposite. We think if we fill kids' heads with facts, they'll turn out to be Christ-followers. It's in the application that life change takes place.

I'm amused when people talk about wanting to take kids "deeper." I've been a Christ-follower for 34 years, and I'm still working on the simple, but very "deep," command to "love your neighbor as yourself." You want to know what deep is? Deep is application. Deep is living out what you've been taught. You want to take kids "deep"? Then show them how to live out what they've learned!

Teach relationship over retention. I'm more concerned about teaching a boy how to spend time talking with Jesus than I am about teaching him the names of the 12 disciples. I'm more concerned about teaching a girl how to grow closer to Jesus by reading his Word than I am about teaching her how many stones David picked up to fight Goliath. Retention of facts doesn't change a child's life…a heart relationship with Jesus does!

Pray for God to touch the hearts of the children in your ministry. It is God who moves truth from the head to the heart. He is the one who transforms kids into heart followers of Christ. Ask God to make his Word come alive in the hearts of the children in your ministry. Immerse your lessons and teaching in prayer.

Make sure your aim is at the heart…not just the head!

—Dale

The Sorority

What do you do when you don't know where to start?

Assess the situation. When I began in ministry, I was privileged to lead a small team of women, all of whom had been in our church's children's ministry for anywhere from six months to three years. The previous children's pastor had left, and they had been doing it on their own for about six months. They did a great job for the most part, but they had faced some pretty big obstacles.

First, without clear leadership, they made many decisions by committee. This led to delays in execution because everyone had ideas. Another obstacle was that the team had no one fighting on their behalf with leadership, no clear representation. These women were highly competent. They simply were not positioned for maximum success. As I got to know them, their strengths and weaknesses, I made some quick changes.

Give ownership. After identifying all of our responsibilities, I assigned each team member to specifically lead and oversee all aspects of one or more areas. This instantly gave them an accountability and authority they previously lacked.

Empower. Next, I empowered them to make decisions in their respective areas. No longer would they have to check with everyone else before they could act. Team members were to assess their individual areas, decide a course of action, and implement it—without discussing it with anyone on the team other than me.

Schedule and perform regular checkups. We regularly evaluated our ministry and made changes wherever necessary. One of our team members decided she needed to stay home with her kids, and when she quit, it left a gap. Rather than simply filling that gap, we looked at all of our tasks and responsibilities, assessed our current staff and their gifts and passions, and we restructured the team accordingly. After the restructure, we were able to clearly define what we didn't have covered, and then we could hire accordingly. This technique proved successful time and again.

Learn from mistakes. When you entrust a team member and he or she fails, always support the person publicly and reinforce your belief in him or her. Failure is an event, not a person. Perform correction and strategy adjustments in private.

Embrace change. What works today may not work a year from now. Train your team to remain fluid.

You're all in this together. You must be your team's voice, and many times you may have to take the battlefield on their behalf. If you do, over time you'll see a team emerge that's fiercely loyal to you and to the vision.

—**Scott**

Listen to Parents!

Successful organizations listen to those they serve. They take time to get feedback, insight, and ideas from their customers so they can make their product or service better. This principle can translate straight into your ministry. Your ministry will benefit tremendously by listening to the parents you serve.

A great way to listen to parents is through focus groups. Focus groups shout to parents that you want to partner with them in their kids' spiritual development. Focus groups help you see your children's ministry through other eyes. Focus groups help you discover what is working and what needs to be adjusted or changed. Focus groups will let you know the struggles and challenges parents are facing. Focus groups will give you insight and ideas that you won't get anywhere else.

Here are some practical tips for implementing parent focus groups in your ministry.

Make focus groups age-specific. In other words, hold a focus group for parents of preschoolers, one for parents of elementary kids, and so on.

Decide who to invite. I recommend inviting 8 to 10 parents. Invite a variety of parents—those who have been attending your church for a long time and those who just started attending. Those who have been believers for a long time and new believers. Single parents as well as couples.

Start the meeting with prayer. Ask God to lead the discussion.

Dive into discussion. Create an environment where parents feel free to give their ideas and opinions. Have a list of questions and topics prepared to discuss. Here are some examples.

- How can we partner with you in your child's spiritual development?

- What would you like to see your child taught from God's Word?

- What do you want your child to learn and live out?

- What are some areas in which you'd like to see your child grow spiritually?

- What are some issues and challenges that you see your child facing in the culture right now? How can we partner with you to help navigate through these issues?

- What are some challenges and struggles you are facing as a parent right now? How can we help?

- How can we make your child's experience at church better?

- What's working well in our children's ministry? What are some areas we can improve?

- How can we communicate with you better?

Accept all feedback with a positive attitude. Learn from everything that is said. Constructive criticism is good. Even in the most extreme criticism there is usually at least a grain of truth. Don't get defensive. Remember the parents are on your side. They want to make the ministry better just as you do.

Create an action plan to implement ideas you and your team gain from the meeting. Keep parents in the loop as you act upon their feedback and ideas.

Many parents in your ministry would love to partner with you. They're just waiting for you to ask!

—**Dale**

60

The Survey

Our team was driving to a children's ministry conference, and I decided to take advantage of the time in the car. We had three cars and three teams. Each person was to complete a survey I provided and then share their answers with their team members. When we arrived later that night, we would gather for a planning session and kick it off with a game.

I would read the responses from the survey. The team that could identify the most responses from their team and the team members who gave them won a prize. (Actually I don't think there was a prize. Prizes cost money, right? But they still got to win! And in our competitive group, that was prize enough.)

Little did I realize the impact this exercise would have on our team. We had so much fun. We got to know each other in new ways. People still talk about that years later. The rules and the survey follow:

Team Challenge. To get to know each other better, the following activity has been planned for your vehicle. Spend as much or as little time as you wish on this activity. Drive safely, and I'll see you at the conference!

Objective. Discover new, unknown facts about your car mates. Retain that information for a quiz that will be administered upon arrival. During the quiz, no notes, cheats, or verbal help will be allowed. The team who can share the most details of each member of their team will emerge victorious! Drivers must have someone else in the vehicle complete their form on their behalf and are excluded from participation in the challenge. Teammates must know their driver's information. Each person has been provided a pen. Each person should complete this questionnaire personally, with exact wording that must be replicated by his or her teammates during the quiz. You may trade notes or go over them verbally during the visit. You may not duplicate or omit answers to gain an advantage—all answers must be honest and individual. Have fun, and get to know each other!

The Survey

1. Name
2. My favorite color is
3. Maiden name [middle name for guys and unmarried]
4. My pet's name as a child
5. I have a tattoo/I do not have a tattoo. (Circle one.)
6. My all-time favorite movie is
7. If I were an animal, it would be a/an
8. In my heart of hearts, I do/do not believe that my pet will be in heaven. (Circle one.)
9. The most influential person in my life besides my parents is/was:
10. Confidentially, my favorite worship pastor is
11. One book (besides the Bible) that had a profound impact on my life was
12. I have considered/am considering/would consider/would not consider plastic surgery. (Circle one.)
13. If I could change one thing about my physical appearance, it would be (Yes, I know you are confident and have accepted who you are! Answer it.)
14. If I were to describe my relationship with Christ in one word, that word would be
15. On a scale of 1 (horrible) to 10 (unbelievable) I would rate Pastor Craig's looks as
16. My favorite of the four seasons is

Change it up as necessary. Use it with your team. Have your volunteers try it at your next training event. Have fun. But be ready:

The results of this survey game might just rock your world.

—Scott

61

The Core!

The mission statement of our children's ministry is "Connecting kids and families to Christ and helping them become followers of him." Plain and simple, that's why we exist. This mission is the engine that drives us. But inside the engine are 10 pistons that give the engine the power to move us forward. Ten core values that make the mission become a reality. Ten core values that help us accomplish our mission. Here they are…

1. Making church a fun and exciting experience for kids. (Psalm 122:1)

We believe that kids should have tons of fun at church. In other words, kids enjoy being there. I have met lots of people over the years who won't attend church because they were made to go as a child. You don't have to make someone go where they enjoy being! I've never heard anyone say "I'm not going to Disney World because I was made to go as a child." The problem was they were placed in an environment that was irrelevant to their needs as a child. It was boring for them, and the impact still lingers today even as an adult.

I often listen to new families as they pick up their children. Guess what is the number-one question parents ask their child. "Did you have fun today?" We are committed to helping children experience God in a fun, age-appropriate way. In fact, we even named one of our environments "The Fun Factory…Where God Makes Church Fun!"

2. Reaching children and their families who don't have a relationship with Christ. (Luke 19:10)

We are committed to reaching out to those who don't have a relationship with God. Our heart must beat with the heart of Jesus. He wants everyone to be a part of his kingdom. There is nothing more important than this.

We must intentionally and strategically share the good news with families. People are seeking…we have the answer…it's what matters most.

In the next four weeks, our kids will pass out 30,000 church invite cards to their friends, neighbors, schoolmates, and family members. We are believing that hundreds of new kids and families will come to Christ because of it.

3. Partnering with families in their child's spiritual growth. (Deuteronomy 6:5-9)

Parents are called to be the primary spiritual leader in their children's lives. We are committed to partnering with them in this endeavor. We provide resources, family discussion guides, focus groups, and more. We ask parents to attend our new believers class for kids with their children and be the major influence on the journey.

This year when the kids came back from camp, we asked parents to meet with us 30 minutes before the kids arrived back. We shared with them highlights of the week and gave them an outline of what their children learned at camp with a discussion guide. Intentional partnerships like this can make the difference.

4. Helping kids build meaningful relationships through small groups. (John 13:34-35)

Cool room environments may get kids in the door of your church, but it's relationships that will keep them. We are committed to helping kids connect with other kids, caring leaders, and God through small groups of six to eight kids. In a small group, kids find acceptance, love, and belonging. In a small group, kids can share about their week. In a small group, kids can pray together. In a small group, kids can grow in their faith. In a small group, kids can have a leader that personally knows them and invests in their lives.

5. Creatively presenting the timeless truths of the Bible in an engaging, culturally relevant, and age-appropriate way. (1 Corinthians 9:19-23)

The truths of the Bible never change. But we must be committed to packaging those timeless truths in a way that today's kids can connect with. McDonalds is a great example of packaging to connect with kids. The first Happy Meal came out in 1979. It was in a kid-friendly, decorated box that

contained a hamburger, fries, drink, and a toy. Today's Happy Meal still comes in a box that contains a hamburger, fries, drink, and a toy. But the box decorations and toys have changed many times since 1979. The box decoration and toy will always be a reflection of something that is currently relevant in kid culture. Food is basically the same…packaging changes. McDonalds has learned the secret to connect with kids over the years. Package your decorations and toy to match what is culturally relevant in their culture.

As children's ministries we must make sure our packaging of the truth is not stuck in the year 1979. We must creatively bring the truth to kids in the language of their current culture.

6. Teaching life-application, not just information. (James 1:22)

We are committed to helping kids live out what they learn. We want to see them become "doers" of the word and not just "hearers." It's not just about compiling a list of Bible facts in their heads. It's about seeing them become active Christ-followers because of applied truth. Each week we intentionally challenge kids to live out the truth we have taught them. The challenge is put in writing and sent home with them.

7. Providing a safe and secure environment. (Psalm 4:8)

We live in a scary world. Things have changed since I was a child. As a fourth-grader I had a paper route and rode my bike several miles early in the morning. I wouldn't think of allowing my child to do that in our city. Recently a child was abducted just a few miles from our house.

Providing a safe and secure environment must be a top priority. Volunteers must be carefully selected and go through background checks. No adult is ever allowed to be alone in a room with a child. Children must be checked in and out of classrooms through a secure process.

Parents must know that their children are safe and secure in your care. The church should be a safe haven where kids and parents can worship without fear of something happening.

8. Empowering a team of people to use their gifts in ministry. (Ephesians 4:11-12)

Show me an effective children's ministry and I will show you a great team of volunteers. We must be committed to enlisting, equipping, and releasing people to do the work of the ministry. Each week a major part of our staff meeting is going through a list of people we are going after to join our team. We also spend a major part of our time and resources on equipping and empowering our team.

9. Equipping kids to reach and serve their generation for Christ. (Matthew 28:19-20)

We believe that God can use the kids in our ministry to make a major difference…not just when they get older, but now!

We were raising money for a new children's building. I challenged the kids to sacrifice and be a part of it. One of the third-grade boys had planned a trip to Sea World with his family. When he heard about the need, he went, on his own, to his parents and asked if they could cancel the trip and use the money to help build the new children's building. Of course, his parents were blown away by their child's heart to make a difference and said yes. God used this young boy to challenge many other people in the church to give.

The kids in our ministries can make a difference. Pour into them and release them to reach and serve their generation!

10. Excellence! (Ecclesiastes 9:10)

The core value of excellence should be reflected in everything we do as children's ministries. Programming…events…communication…print pieces… videos…it should all be done with a high commitment to excellence.

I love Lexus' motto: "The relentless pursuit of perfection." It's not just a fancy tagline in its advertising efforts. It's a philosophy the automotive company lives by in everything it does.

No, our children's ministries aren't going to do everything perfectly. But we should constantly be pursuing it, looking for ways to improve, and making things better.

IDEAS

- Put your core values in print for all to see.
- Take each new team member through the core values.
- Take time to teach on at least one core value at each of your training sessions/team meetings.

- If you send an information packet to guests or new families, include the core values as a print piece.
- Use the core values to evaluate your ministry on a regular basis.

These core values are empowering us to make a difference in our community. Discover your set of core values, live by them, and watch God do great things!

—**Dale**

62

Through the Cracks

Good Old-Testament Hebrew boys Shadrach, Meshach, and Abednego offer us amazing insight into what children, properly nurtured, are capable of. Ripped from God-fearing homes and dropped into a pagan palace, they faced constant obstacles. Eat this. Do as you're told. Worship or die. With no visible reason to hope, no future, they could easily have given in.

But their resolve was unshakable. Shadrach, Meshach, and Abednego peered through the cracks in the wall of their prison, and they saw light, *the* light. Where does faith like that come from?

Proverbs 22:6 says, "Direct your children onto the right path, and when they are older, they will not leave it."

Shadrach, Meshach, and Abednego were the next generation in an entire legacy of faith, one passed down to them lovingly, with conviction, from their elders. These boys' commitment wasn't based on popular opinion or circumstances. It was rooted deep, in one simple, unshakable belief: that God's Word is true. Oh that we may see children like that in our ministries in this generation! Our primary ministry is to partner with parents in pointing their children toward Jesus.

Children are not subordinate Christians. For too long, the church has viewed children as subordinate, even lesser, Christians. Scripture disagrees. Every promise made to adult believers is 100 percent true for *all* believers, regardless of age. When we pursue God, when we seek him, he pursues us in return. Does that cease to be true below a certain age? Show me.

Neil T. Anderson says in *The Bondage Breaker* that every verse in the Bible has only three possible elements: If it's a truth, believe it; if it's a promise, accept it; if it's a command, obey it. (Try it! It's true.) So besides just the promises, children are equally required to follow scriptural direction. "Choose today who you will serve." "Love the Lord your God with all your heart, soul, mind, and strength." We must lead them appropriately, sharing that responsibility with them and bearing one another's burdens together with them, as co-heirs with them in God's promises.

We have the added responsibility to stand up for their rights within our own ministry structure. As co-heirs, they're every bit as entitled to ministry resources. In many cases, they need it even more...

Lay a foundation early, or risk missing the chance. George Barna's research indicates that the moral foundation in a person's life is established in the preteen years. In children's ministry, we have the opportunity to grab their attention as infants and assist their parents in ushering them into a strong, lifelong faith. We have a responsibility to teach our kids how to explore their own hearts, to confirm their faith for themselves. This is a precious gift. We must rise to the challenge. We need to teach their parents how to teach them, too, to reinforce the truth in their lives.

Children have the faith to believe. Jesus said (more than once), "You want an example of what your 'adult faith' should look like? Look no farther than the faith of a child." (I'm paraphrasing—but only a little.) Do you remember a time in your life before you learned to doubt? Do you remember when you heard God's Word and just believed it? We are surrounded by a great cloud of little witnesses who operate in that kind of faith. What if we could tap that same faith they have? What would our prayers—not to mention our lives—look like if we simply believed as they do?

We have to act now, while they're still young, consistently pointing our kids toward the truth that God's Word is an unwavering fact in *their* lives, too. We also have to empower them to stand alone, for those inevitable times when we're not going to be there with them. Teach them to look through the cracks and to see the light for themselves!

—Scott

More Serving Positions = More Volunteers!

"So pray to the Lord who is in charge of the harvest; ask him to send more workers into his fields."

—Matthew 9:38

Do you need more volunteers? I know I do. The truth is, no matter what size church you are in, you will probably always need more volunteers. Especially if you are reaching kids and families and are growing.

One thing I've discovered is more serving positions equals more volunteers! Perhaps you currently only have 10 volunteers. No matter how hard you try, you can't seem to get any more. What if you added some more positions for people to serve in? Increase the number of service positions, and you will increase the number of volunteers. It sounds simple, but it's very effective. Here are ways to get more people involved by creating more serving positions.

Make your dream list of serving positions. What if you had an unlimited number of volunteers? What new positions would you create for them? Go ahead...act like you do and make the list. Create a spreadsheet or diagram of all the serving positions you could ever want. Place a blank under each position. Then obey Matthew 9:38 and ask God to fill the blanks with people.

Create lots of "entry" positions. This is one of the keys to getting lots of new people on your team. Many people are hesitant about volunteering because they don't feel like they can teach, sing, or lead. Creating positions that are easy to do opens a door that many of these people will walk through.

Lots of people are extremely busy and are hesitant to serve because of the time commitment. Creating positions that require a shorter time commitment can help people make the decision to serve. Here's an example. I've had businessmen in our church who traveled frequently and had very hectic schedules. Normally this would have kept them from serving. But I created positions where they could serve once or twice a month for an hour. This enabled them to step up and join the team.

The cool thing is that many times God will raise up people in the "easy" positions to greater responsibility in your ministry. Some of the greatest leaders I have known in children's ministry started out in "easy" positions. Over time, God put a desire in their hearts to do more. They got in the room and experienced the joy of serving kids. Their spiritual gifts blossomed. Their schedules changed and they had more time to serve. They became movers and shakers in children's ministry. People who started as greeters became teachers. People who started passing out papers became small-group leaders.

Karina started out acting in some of our skits. It's been awesome watching God helping her grow. She now leads our drama ministry and spends many hours each week practicing and coordinating the schedule. Here is an e-mail she recently sent to us.

"Thanks for all you do! Getting involved in The Fun Factory and drama team has been such a blessing in my life. I don't know where or when it happened, but between the awesome team, witnessing firsthand the children's pure faith, or hearing and trying to live out your messages and the dramas, for the first time I really feel connected to God in a real way and that I have a genuine relationship with Christ. Thanks for your encouragement. You guys rock!"

Write a job description for every position. What are the exact duties of the position? How often will people serve? How much time will it take? How much preparation will be involved? Answering these questions up front will help you place more people on your team.

Let people know about specific positions. How can people serve if they don't know what the positions are? Spread the word! Distribute a list of the new positions. Mail the list to parents. Pass it out at a new-members class. Make a "Top 10 Easy Ways to Serve and Make a Big Impact" list, and put it in the weekend program guide. People are ready to serve...they just need to know there are positions that will fit their schedules and gifts.

Adding more serving positions doesn't mean you have to add more programming or events. It simply means you are adding more positions to enhance your current programming or events.

There are people in your church waiting to serve in your children's ministry. You just haven't created a position for them yet. Expand your service positions and watch God expand your team.

—Dale

To Everything There Is a Season

If you randomly asked 100 Americans where the line "to everything there is a season" came from, sadly, I imagine more would think it was from the pen of Pete Seeger and made famous by The Byrds in the '60s than its actual origin: the book of Ecclesiastes:

"For everything there is a season, a time for every activity under heaven. A time to be born and a time to die. A time to plant and a time to harvest. A time to kill and a time to heal. A time to tear down and a time to build up. A time to cry and a time to laugh. A time to grieve and a time to dance. A time to scatter stones and a time to gather stones. A time to embrace and a time to turn away. A time to search and a time to quit searching. A time to keep and a time to throw away. A time to tear and a time to mend. A time to be quiet and a time to speak. A time to love and a time to hate. A time for war and a time for peace" (Ecclesiastes 3:1-8).

What a wonderful promise from God's Word. Seasons come and seasons go. Nothing's permanent. If you're crying, laughter will return. If you're grieving, joy will find its way again. There's a time for every activity under heaven. Throughout your ministry career, you'll surely experience many seasons.

Planting. Plan and prepare.

You might need to find a new curriculum, build a new facility, train volunteers…even start a new church. Planting is laying the groundwork for your future reward. In our experience, this is a difficult time, requiring a lot of hard work. But it's also a sweet time for relationships. This kind of work bonds people who have worked together—cleaning, painting, writing—whatever the task was. A planting season is a time you have to faithfully trust God and know that in due time you'll reap the fruits of what you and your team have sown. One day, you'll reflect on planting as "the good old days."

Pruning. Pain, loss, correction, or separation.

You *will* experience loss. It's inevitable. Maybe a faithful volunteer or staff member will move away. Maybe you'll suffer pain at the death of a vision. Maybe your responsibilities will change. Maybe you'll simply make a mistake and suffer the consequences. Pruning is necessary and critical. Pruning is the most painful season, but it often yields the most tangible, real results, both in our lives and in our ministries. God's Word is true. Joy will return. Your mistakes can be made right. God promises to correct those he loves. The very things that our enemy tries to twist for evil, God will use for our good. The season of pruning can teach the toughest, most lasting lessons, empower us with the greatest resolve, and lock in our most cherished memories.

Harvesting. Reap the rewards of your labors.

It's time to rejoice! Enjoy the fruits of your labors. Celebrate God's goodness in your life and in the lives of your team members. Thank the Lord for everything he's done. Give him all the glory and honor and praise. Thank him, knowing that all good and perfect gifts come from him!

Wherever you are, be encouraged. Plant the seedlings of your vision with faithfulness, and allow God to give the increase. Persevere through the pruning, knowing that when your faith is tested, your endurance will have a chance to grow. If we don't grow weary, if we don't give up, God promises that we'll reap a harvest (Galatians 6:9).

Seasons change. Influence and leadership are temporary gifts. Use them wisely to accomplish his will in your life and in your ministry.

—**Scott**

Many times we have the mentality in children's ministry that "if you're breathing, you can serve." This kind of thinking will never build an excellent team. When someone wants to serve in your ministry, don't immediately say yes. It's important to sit down first and have a one-on-one interview. Schedule a time to meet. Buy a coffee. Then go through the following interview...

Thank the person for coming. Explain that the interview is part of the process of becoming a team member. You want to learn more and find the best ministry fit for the person.

Ask these questions to get to know the person:

- Can you tell me about your background?
- Can you tell me about your family?
- Where do you work?
- What are your hobbies and interests?
- How did you become a Christ-follower?
- When and how did you start attending our church?

Ask these questions to gain an understanding of the person's spiritual maturity:

- How would you describe your relationship with Christ?
- How do you grow in your relationship with Christ?
- How has God worked in your life recently?

Ask these questions to find out what area might be a good ministry fit:

- What would those who know you best say are your best qualities?

- What do you feel are your greatest strengths?

- What areas do you need to work on?

- Are you more of an extrovert or an introvert?

- What about serving in ministry excites you?

- Is there a specific position you are interested in serving in?

- Do you have any past training or experience in serving?

- Are there any areas of serving that intimidate you or that you feel unsure about?

- How busy is your life? Is there anything in your schedule or life that might hinder your ability to serve?

Ask these questions to decide if the person is emotionally capable of being in leadership:

- Are there presently any issues that you are working through that have not been fully resolved (family, drugs, alcohol, finances, sexual matters, depression)?

- Can you tell me about the current condition of your home life (kids, spouse, roommates)? Is your spouse supportive of you serving?

- Have you been through any major life changes in the last year (major move, marriage, divorce, loss of loved one, sickness)? How are you doing with the adjustment?

Allow the person to ask questions or voice concerns. Listen carefully and discuss issues.

Don't turn the interview into an interrogation; make it conversational. Jot down brief notes, and go back later if you want to write more details.

If you feel the person qualifies to join the team, provide an application and do a background check. (See Idea 47.) If red flags have popped up, kindly say that you feel he or she would be a better fit in another ministry. Say this in a positive way, and encourage the person to look for another ministry in which to serve. If you see major red flags and you don't feel he or she should

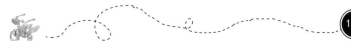

be serving anywhere, then obviously don't say anything about another ministry. Thank the person for coming and pray with him or her before leaving.

Don't underestimate the importance of an initial interview. Don't rush through or skip questions. Take time to interview thoroughly. The interview will set the tone for the person's service with you. Down the road, you'll be glad you took the time to do it well—or you'll be wishing you had.

—**Dale**

Trust Your Team

You can't make a real impact—or start seeing real change—until you learn to duplicate yourself. For example, as your role evolves and grows, your responsibilities will also scale up accordingly. You'll find yourself tied up in meetings, on the phone, on the computer. But you have so much to do! Identify others who can do with excellence the things that you no longer have time for. Better yet, find people who can do those things better than you could.

Share your shoes. How would your senior pastor perform onstage in your elementary service? Be honest. It's OK. How would *you* do on the "grown-up stage"? The answers are both probably "Not so great." That's how it's supposed to be. You each do your own thing.

Identify what only you can do. As the leader, there are certain things that only you can do. Maybe it's ministry visits, meeting with leadership, or handling a disgruntled parent or volunteer. Identify what those *specific* things are. Be wise. Prioritize. Make the most of your time.

Delegate your weaknesses. If you can't quickly reconcile a budget or write a mailer paragraph, find someone who can. Better still, find someone who's (a) great at it and (b) enjoys it. Seek win-wins. Set your expectations clearly. Just because you're not doing it doesn't mean you should neglect it. Ultimately, you'll have to answer for all the work under your charge. You're not delegating the responsibility…just the execution.

Enable failure. Encourage it if you have to. Promise your team that if they'll play within your leadership, with integrity, always giving their best work, then you'll always publicly support their efforts. You can handle any adjustment, correction, or reproof appropriately: in private. Dirty laundry belongs in the hamper, not in the living room. Create an environment where it's safe to reach big…and to fail just as big.

Get out of the way. You can tell when you have the right people. How? Because they'll exceed your personal ability. Water your team. Then let it flourish. Let it grow.

The people serving with you want to be a part of big things. They want to please you. They want to succeed. Let them. Then you can focus on the things you really need to, secure in the knowledge that your team's got your back.

—**Scott**

When it comes to children's ministry…looks do matter. The "look" of your children's ministry will directly affect the impact you have in your community. Here are some key areas that can make your children's ministry look great to kids and families.

Create a name for your children's ministry. It's important to name your children's ministry. Don't just call it the "children's department." A fun and exciting name says your children's ministry is a cool place for kids.

Keep the name short and simple. Make it easy for kids and parents to remember. Consider tying it to the name of your church. Our church is called Central Christian Church, so we named our children's ministry "Central Kidz." We added the "z" to make it fun and appealing to kids.

Create a name for your age environments. Disneyland is a great example. *Disneyland* is the overall name of the park. But inside Disneyland, you have different environments. There is Frontierland, Tomorrowland, Adventureland, and so on. Each of these areas is clearly marked when you enter. They each have a unique feel and attraction. This causes you to feel anticipation and excitement as you transition into each area.

By creating a unique look and feel for each age environment, you will fill kids with anticipation and excitement as they grow and transition. Central Kidz is the overall name of our children's ministry. But inside Central Kidz are three unique environments: Adventure Island (preschool), The Fun Factory (early elementary), and Gear Zone (upper elementary/preteen).

Create a slogan. Nike…Just do it!

G.E.…We bring good things to life.

M&M's…The milk chocolate melts in your mouth, not in your hands.

These are all examples of effective slogans. They are simple statements that convey big-impact thoughts. The slogan for your children's ministry should shout out what you want to be known for. Our children's ministry slogan is "The Place for Kids and Families."

Add your slogan as a tag line under your children's ministry name and logo. Let families see the slogan on everything. Placing it constantly before them will embed it in their minds.

Create a logo. A great logo is vital for your children's ministry's look. Don't take shortcuts in this area. Make your logo first-class. Spend the time and resources to make your logo scream excellence.

Make your logo kid-friendly. Look through the eyes of a child, and make it fun and colorful. Great logos don't have to cost a fortune. Check with local graphic artists or look online. There are hundreds of companies that can give you an excellent logo at a good price. (We use plainjoestudios.com.)

Create a mascot. Businesses use mascots to connect with kids. (Ever been to Chuck E. Cheese?) A mascot can be a great way to connect kids to your children's ministry. Mascot costumes can be bought or designed. A quality mascot can definitely add a first-class look to your children's ministry.

Use your mascot as a greeter. Incorporate it in your services. Use your mascot on your printed materials. Mascots work best for preschool and early elementary children. Our preschool environment has a mascot monkey called Pax. Pax is a puppet who comes out and interacts with the kids each week. He is an important part of the service.

Have quality printed pieces. Looks matter when it comes to printed materials. Everything you hand out should be done with excellence. Brochures, take-home papers, posters, and lesson plans should reflect quality. Quality doesn't always have to mean full-color. No matter the size of your budget, you can produce materials that are neat, proofread, and laid out well.

Create kid-friendly environments. Buildings and great-looking facilities don't keep kids coming. Relationships keep kids coming to church. But… great-looking facilities will bring new kids and families in the door so you can build relationships with them. Whether you like it nor not, a new family instantly judges your children's ministry by your facilities.

Don't be sidetracked by those who say it's a waste of money to create kid-friendly facilities. It's one of the best investments you will ever make in your children's ministry. A great-looking kid facility will be a kid and family magnet!

—**Dale**

VBX

VBX: This ain't your grandma's vacation Bible school!

Xtreme Days. Live alligators and cheetahs in an Extreme Pet Show. Exotic cars power-sliding in an Extreme Car Show and Demonstration. And me, drinking live goldfish onstage. (OK, that's not extreme. But I *did* it!) BMX bikers hopped off a short ramp...and over my head as I spoke. Motorcyclists did wheelies the length of the parking lot. A motocross superstar jumped a fire engine. Every day was literally *extreme!* More than 2,000 kids came the first day. Each day, attendance climbed higher than the day before. Literally hundreds of children embraced the love of Christ for the first time, and we saw them make decisions to give their hearts to him. It was extreme. It was turbocharged.

Fact: Kids don't like school. Working with kids on the weekends, it occurred to us—kids don't like school. It's true! Kids go to school because they *have to,* and they celebrate when they're out. Why do we call these events vacation Bible *school* and Sunday *school?* Especially during the summer, do kids really want to go to more "school"? We changed the name. VBS—vacation Bible school—became VBX...vacation Bible *xperience.* For the tagline, we went with "VBX—This Ain't Your Grandma's Vacation Bible School."

Ask...Why did we do it? We had three answers to this question: (1) provide one week of activities for the children of our church, (2) provide an opportunity for guests and families in our community to come together for fun and friendships, and (3) point everyone who attends toward Jesus.

Ask...What's the point? We wanted to teach children that an extreme love prompted God to give up his only Son, in turn producing *extreme* passion in us to live for him, in these days—extreme days. There was our name. TobyMac had a killer hit with the same name from a few years before, so that was a no-brainer. We had the plan. Now we had to pull it off.

Pull out all the stops. God had to provide. We prayed for his blessing, then we pursued everything we'd need to do it right. Companies and individuals donated thousands of dollars' worth of products, money, and other things, supplementing our already-generous leadership. Little by little, the dream came alive.

If your traditions aren't broken...break them. VBX was seeker-driven community outreach, targeting literally thousands of local kids. We didn't have room for the numbers we wanted. Rather than "solving" this "problem" by excluding kids outside the church, we simply scheduled most events outside. (Also, cars and motorcycles are bad for carpet.) Rather than a single kitchen, we strategically scattered snack stations outside. Kids went to whichever line was shortest. Crafts for that many kids was unrealistic. So we taught them a dance to a worship song instead.

In my previous career, I was a realtor. To promote our event, I decided we'd print simple, cheap yard signs, like political signs, with "VBX," the dates, and a website address. We gave away literally thousands at church. Within weeks, they blanketed the city's neighborhoods and businesses. The website had all the details.

As awesome as VBX turned out, the following summer...we didn't do it. Of the purposes we had identified—a week of activities, local community outreach, pointing to Jesus—we couldn't do justice to the first two goals with the multi-campus vision our church had grown into. Every locality couldn't have the same experience. That call hurt. But it was the right one.

What have you allowed to remain as it was? What have you sacrificed to maintain the programs and status quo that preceded you? Where do you need to believe God for new results? Whatever those areas might be, go extreme!

—Scott

You Need a Good Coaching Team!

"Talent wins games, but teamwork and intelligence wins championships."

—Michael Jordan

If you're going to grow your children's ministry, then you have to develop a good coaching team. You must realize that you can't provide care for everyone by yourself. One person can only effectively care for four or five people. Beyond that you lose true ministry touch.

Many churches and ministries fail to grasp this concept. The people expect the pastor or staff member in charge of the ministry to do everything. As a result the growth of the church or ministry is hindered. The opposite is true when you develop volunteer leaders who come alongside you and help coach the ministry.

Develop volunteer leaders who lead other volunteers. Appoint volunteer leaders to be coaches for four to five volunteers. The leaders you appoint as coaches should have the following qualities:

- Loyalty to the mission
- Faithfulness
- Dependability
- Good people skills
- Encouragement
- Experience in the area of service

An example is our small-group coaches. A small group coach cares for four to five small-group leaders. They call them, pray with them, meet their needs, encourage them, mentor them, and help them grow in their ministry position. When the small-group leader needs something, he or she calls the coach instead of the staff person.

Pour yourself into your coaches, who will in turn pour themselves into the volunteers they lead. Meet regularly with your coaches. Share key information with them. Get feedback from them. Teach your coaches key leadership principles and ideas that they can teach to the volunteers they lead.

Show me a great team, and I will show you a great group of coaches. Show me a great children's ministry, and I will show you a great group of people leading together...each contributing to the overall strength of the leadership team!

—**Dale**

70

Walmart, Here We Come

What are you willing to do to help this generation of kids know Christ? What will you do to grab their attention? What will you do to keep them engaged? The best answer always points to relationship. Nothing replaces the human factor. But that can't be all.

In this age, we have to do whatever we can—short of sin, of course—to bring children in, keep them, and point them toward Christ. One idea is a rewards and incentives program. In our younger elementary ministry, we reward kids for their accomplishments. Each child receives an account, where he or she can earn and save Toon Town Bucks.

We modeled our incentive portion after the prize counters at Chuck E. Cheese or Dave and Buster's. Toon Town's "Good News Stand" displays all the "prizes" a kid can save for.

But brace yourself for criticism. The use of incentives is a hotly debated topic in children's ministry. Some believe that kids will repeat verses, bring friends, and otherwise strive to fulfill your hopes for them solely in an effort to gain rewards, sacrificing true learning along the way.

It works for us. But you'll need to make your own decision. Watch out, Walmart. We're coming for prizes.

—**Scott**

71

High Commitment = High-Quality Leaders!

More than 18 years ago, I stood at a wedding altar and made a commitment to my wife, Pamela. That day I made a commitment to love, honor, and cherish her for life. Eighteen years later, we are more committed and more in love with each other than ever before. We look forward to spending the rest of our lives together.

A serious relationship means you have made some serious commitments. When it comes to our team members serving, we should expect them to make some serious commitments. We should raise the bar. If you expect high commitment up front, it will produce high-quality leaders.

People want to commit their lives to something greater than themselves. As you share with them the eternal importance of what they will be doing, most people will respond to the challenge.

When someone joins our team, we ask them to sign a team member covenant. We go over the commitment with them so they will have a clear understanding of what we are asking of them. Here's what we ask…

- Make a one-year commitment to serve in Family Ministries.

- Attend a worship service each weekend and First Wednesday.

- Keep yourself spiritually healthy and growing through prayer, Bible study, and accountability.

- Champion unity in the church and agree not to teach or practice anything that is contrary to the teaching of our church.

- Enthusiastically participate in regular leadership development opportunities provided by the ministry.

- Seek the counsel of their ministry leader if they have any struggles or challenges that might affect the ministry.

- Share any changes in their personal information that might have an impact on the ministry.

Team members are wholeheartedly committed to the greatest cause in the world! Raise the bar! Challenge people to step up! Teach them that God deserves our best. They will respond, and you will begin to see high-quality leaders emerge!

—**Dale**

My name is Scott Alan Werner, and I'm a children's pastor. *Hi, Scott.* Hi. My parents named me after their senior pastor's sons, Scott and Alan. My initials spell "SAW." My dad used to call me "Jabbo." When I was a kid, everybody called me "Scotty." Why does this matter? I'll answer that question with a question: What's the simplest, most profound way to define relationship? (Hint: The answer is "nicknames.")

Define your relationships. Maybe you're in a new position and you really don't know anyone. Maybe you've been part of your church since it started. You have to get past the business, past the meetings, past the programs... and into relationship. You have to delineate between boss and friend, both for those who lead you and for those you lead.

But if it works, if things go well, then the people you work with will become some of the most important people in your life. One way we define culture in our ministry is by relationship.

Assign nicknames where appropriate...and embrace your own. I met my pastor when I was about 20 years old. He was leading a Bible study that I visited with a girl I was dating. A few years later, I learned through a mutual friend that he had started a new church. We visited and reconnected, and you can probably guess the rest.

My pastor and I share a mutual friend from about that same time named Scott. Scott's 6'5", and he played college basketball. We call him "Stretch" or "Stretchy." My pastor's name is Craig Groeschel. I call him "Rev" or "Groesch." Over the years, these two have called me just about every name in the book. My nickname progression looks like this:

Werner, my last name, led to...

Weiner, a variation on my last name, led to...

Weiner Dog, a variation on the variation on my last name, led to...

WD, an abbreviation of the variation on the variation on my last name.

When my pastor calls, he starts, "WD..." When I see Scott, it's, "Hey

Stretch…" But this simple exchange represents so much more than the names themselves. It's shorthand, an abbreviated reminder of intimate bonds forged over the years.

Keep on building. Build relationships with parents so they can trust you with spiritual care for their children. Build trusting, equitable relationships with church leadership. Build relationships with kids, so that they'll allow you into their world. Build a relationship with God that makes you more like Jesus. Everything's about relationships.

As you sit through meetings, as you attend training sessions, as you bang your head against the wall, trying to solve the world's problems—look around. Who's standing next to you? What's his or her middle name? Do you know? How's the person's marriage going? Do you know? Are you just going through the motions, or are you serving the Lord alongside others who need you, and who may become some of your closest friends? I pray the latter is true. You need it. So do I.

—**Scott**

Scenario 1

A new family walks up to the door of your children's room. The son is clinging closely to Mom. You can see the hesitancy and anxiety in the child's eyes. The child turns his face away and hides behind Mom. You try your best to persuade the child to come into the room, but to no avail. The parents begin to get frustrated with the child as they try to get him to go into the room. You both finally give up, and the family walks away with the child still clinging closely to Mom.

Scenario 2

A new child is in your room. She sits quietly by herself. She doesn't cry or cause a disturbance. But if you take a second and look into her eyes, you will see someone crying out to be noticed. Someone who wants to find a friend. Someone who wants to fit in. Someone who doesn't want to sit alone.

These are scenarios that happen every week in children's ministries everywhere. But it doesn't have to be that way. You have lots of greeters in your room that could make these new kids feel welcome, loved, and accepted. The greeters just haven't been enlisted and trained yet. You may not have seen them yet because you're looking over their heads. They are around 3 feet tall and full of smiles.

Kids make great greeters and hosts for new kids. Many times a kid can help a new child feel more welcome and comfortable than an adult ever could. Our kid greeters make a huge impact each week. We've seen a big difference in how new kids feel coming into the room since we started our kid-greeter team. Here's how to set up a kid-greeter team.

- Create a name for your kid-greeter team. We call ours "Friendz."

- Make an announcement. Let kids know you're going to be starting a kid-greeter team. Tell them to have their parents sign them up if they are interested in joining.

- Have a training session for the kids. Teach the kids how to be effective greeters. Parents should attend the training session with their children.

- Make name badges for kids who are going to be greeters.

- Have them sign in each week at a specified time before the service begins. Pray with them before the service.

- Meet periodically for continued training.

- If you have a large number of kids wanting to be greeters, you can set up a rotation schedule.

- Assign an adult to be the director of the greeter team. He or she can track attendance, provide hands-on training, and make badges.

Training tips. Here are a few tips to get your training started.

The purpose of Friendz is to help new kids feel welcome, accepted, and comfortable. We encourage greeters to stand inside the door and smile, smile, smile! Boys welcome boys, girls welcome girls.

F.I.S.H.

This is a tool we created to teach our kid greeters how to talk to new kids.

F — **Family** (Ask them about their family, mom, dad, brothers, sisters, grandparents.)

I — **Interests** (Find out what they like to do—skateboarding, swimming, reading, video games.)

S — **School** (Find out where they go to school, their favorite subject.)

H — **Hero** (Find out their favorite sports star, teacher, singer, actor.)

Then a greeter takes the new child around and introduces him or her to some other kids. The greeter will ask if the child wants to play a video game, color, do crafts, watch a video, talk, or just hang out until the service starts.

We also ask the greeters to introduce the child to some of the adult leaders in the room and to stay with the child for the entire service if the child doesn't know anyone else. After the service, the greeter thanks the child for coming and invites him or her to come back next weekend.

—**Dale**

We had two campuses seven miles apart. My pastor and I taught live, leaving ourselves precisely enough time to drive back and forth and arrive at the next service just in time to walk onstage. One message at one campus, then straight to the other. And then back. I was teaching eight times a weekend. (That was nuts.)

At the end of the last experience one weekend, the 1:00 p.m., I was finished. Little did I know, my day was just beginning. As I stepped off the stage, I noticed that I had several missed calls. I checked my first message and froze: "Scott, we've lost a kid."

I was on the phone in an instant, screeching back to the other campus, the one in trouble. On my way there, a staff member filled me in: At the end of the final experience that morning, all the kids were being checked out as usual. One mom couldn't find her child and asked for help. When the volunteers started looking, he…simply…wasn't…there. As concern mounted, the mom began to panic. Understandably. My team sprung into action, involving law enforcement officers on duty.

When I got there, police, church leadership, and the parent were all present. I felt extremely sick, in a way I never had before. Campus leadership was asking me questions I couldn't answer. I tried to calm everybody, reassuring them, "We'll find him."

Nearly two hours later, a call came in. He was safe. He had left with a neighbor's parents and was at their home. That feeling haunts me still. I can't explain how helpless we felt—all of us. That afternoon, I became a different person.

The weakest link in any system is usually…human. We had a great check-in system. A computer software company owner who attended our church created it specifically for us as an act of service. It was—and is—the best system. The child was properly recorded in attendance. We could verify through the computer that he had been there. But no one knew what happened next. No adults remembered the child leaving. All the other kids were gone.

Our system was based on the premise that when you come to get your child, you have to show your matching number to check them out. No kid leaves without a matching number. It always worked without a hitch. Except that once. Later we learned what happened: The child decided he wanted to go home with his neighbor, his best friend. The parents were also close friends. So he simply left with his friend and hopped in their car. The volunteer—just once—didn't verify the tag matched the adult's number. Why? Maybe they recognized them both. Maybe too many kids were streaming out at once. Maybe the importance of security just didn't register with them. We'll never know. But I know this: I never want to be there again.

Security *is* a big deal. Possibly in your church today, there are custody battles raging, disgruntled former spouses fuming, and potential predators lurking. Parents entrust us with their children week in and week out. Second only to pointing them toward Christ, we bear no greater role than to protect them.

God is our shepherd. How many times has the Holy Spirit protected the children in our ministries without our even knowing? Whether it's softening a fall, keeping someone away from the building, or giving you "that feeling" about a new person on your campus, we're surrounded by protection.

Get a system. Use that system. You absolutely should have a system for check-in and checkout. Amazing, affordable systems can help you not only with this task, but can even show you ways to dramatically improve your ministry. Research. Explain to your leadership how important this type of software is. Do whatever it takes to make sure you're doing all you can.

Volunteers will most likely manage your system, so it has to be simple enough for them to catch on and operate quickly. No church is too small. Security must be a top priority for every ministry.

Be consistent. Once you have your system in place, make sure everyone follows the protocol: people you've known your whole life, first-time guests, even your senior pastor's family—every single time, without exception.

As you implement a system, your volunteers will adapt. So will your parents. You just need to make them understand why you have it and how it works. (Tell them my story!) You're only as strong as your weakest link. Make sure all volunteers understand their role in the checkout process, and how one compromise can place a child in harm's way.

So many parents have been mad at me. I mean *really angry.* "But my husband has our tag, and he already went to the car!" *Sorry. You'll have to go get it.* "But you *know* me, Scott! You know who I am! Our kids are on the same soccer team!" *Sorry. Nobody leaves without a tag.* "But we're late for lunch at Grandma's!" *Sorry. Everybody's in a hurry. Our tag system is really quick.*

You name it, I've heard it. Guess what? I…don't…care. Hate me for protecting your child. That's OK. I promise you this: To the best of my and my team's ability, you will never find yourself standing with me and with the police, sobbing, "Where's my child?"

Can you say the same?

—**Scott**

75

Not Another Staff Meeting!

"I have left orders to be awakened at any time in case of national emergency, even if I'm in a cabinet meeting."

—Ronald Reagan

Ever been in a staff meeting and saw someone dozing off? Maybe that person was you. Ever been to a staff meeting where you wanted to jump up and yell "Let me out of here!"? Ever felt like you could get something done if you didn't have to attend so many meetings? I have.

Staff meetings must happen. As a staff, you must come together if you are going to move forward together. Here's the big question: How can you make your staff meeting more than a necessary evil? How can you move beyond just the "ministry minutia" and make it a time of empowering and equipping?

Over the years of participating in and leading staff meetings, we have identified key elements that make a children's ministry staff meeting productive for us. Here they are…

Pick the best time to meet. For us, it's Tuesday morning. Mondays we have a "holy hangover" from the weekend and our brains are not functioning. We also found if we try to meet in the afternoon we get drowsy from the Chinese food we had for lunch. Tuesday mornings we are fresh and ready to go. Find the time when you can mentally be the most productive.

Pick a place to meet. We normally meet in our office, but we also like to meet in a variety of other places such as parks, Starbucks, restaurants, or one of our homes. Occasionally we will meet in a kid-friendly place such as Chuck E. Cheese to get us in kid mode. Meeting outside the office is good to break the routine and spark creative thinking.

Prepare to meet. The person leading the meeting should come well-prepared. Know what you're going to be covering, discussing, and planning.

We always have a meeting agenda. Prepare by turning off cell phones or putting the office phone on hold. Team members should come ready and focused.

Key verse and prayer. We start our meeting by reading and discussing the key verse(s) we will be teaching that weekend. We want the truth embedded in our hearts as we prepare to share it with kids. We then share prayer requests and spend time praying for each other, the coming weekend, and our volunteers. We ask God for his wisdom and creativity as we meet.

Leadership training. We take time to learn and grow. We may watch a DVD, listen to a CD, or share an article or teaching about leadership. Taking time to grow is vital.

Team-building. We take time to grow as a team through a team-building activity or discussion. This deepens our relationships and brings us together.

Book-share. Someone shares from a book he or she was asked to read. Many times we read a book at the same time and discuss it. Normally these are leadership or children's ministry books.

Encouragement notes. We write an encouragement note to a volunteer. We write specific things we appreciate about the person.

Review of the past weekend. We take time to discuss the past weekend services. What worked well? What didn't work well? What are some things we learned? What needs to be adjusted? How can we improve? This helps us get better each week.

Looking ahead. We look at the coming weekend in detail. We walk through the service elements, assignments, and small-group activities. We want everyone to thoroughly know what is planned and be on the same page.

Upcoming events. We look at upcoming events and check the progress of the timelines and assignments.

Volunteer team. This is one of the most important parts of our meeting. We take a look at our current volunteer team. How are they doing? Who is struggling? Who needs extra care right now? Who is growing and shining? Who is ready to be promoted to more responsibility? We make a plan.

Each week we also have a list of potential volunteers that we are going after to join our team. We go through these names one by one and update their status. Have we been able to make contact with them yet? Have we met with them one on one? Have they been to orientation yet? We hold each other accountable for bringing on new team members.

Details. Ah, yes…the details. We know a ministry of excellence is built on managing details well. We track the details to make sure we're taking care of them.

Creative brainstorming. We brainstorm and write creative ideas for upcoming series, lessons, skits, videos, and events. We do this last so the rest of the items on the agenda are not staring at us. We want to be able to focus solely on creativity at this point.

Your staff meeting sets the tone for your week. Don't make it just another meeting. Make it something that team members look forward to. Make it a catalyst for your team, and the results will be obvious.

—**Dale**

76

What's Up, LifeKIDS?

I'll never forget the first day I walked onstage to speak to the kids of our church. That was my first time with them. I'd been offered the job, accepted, and started building my team. But now it was go-time. Now it was real. I was nervous. I knew that God had called me, and I knew that through his calling, I could do this. But something was missing. I needed something to break the ice. Something that belonged just to us, to me and the kids, that would help us connect—something turbocharged! What was I going to do?

Kids are people. Connect with them. As I prepared for this event, surrounded by the excitement that accompanied every aspect of my life at that time, I went to the Lord. Little did I know that his simple answer would become a defining ingredient both in my ministry and in my life.

At the time, a popular commercial featured some knuckleheads who obnoxiously slurred, "What's up?" Everyone knew the commercial, everyone had said it, so I tried it. As I introduced myself to the kids, I told them I wanted them to practice something with me. I told them, "When I yell, 'What's up, LifeKIDS?!' I want you to yell back, 'What's up, Pastor Scott?!' Can you do that?" I got a thunderous affirmation. So we gave it a try. I called out, and they answered. We did it a few times that day, and it worked. They loved yelling in unison. They loved responding louder and louder each time. I had my icebreaker, and we began settling into a routine together.

Be genuine, and be available. As time passed, this one statement grew into so much more. I made the kids this promise: "If you see me anywhere… *anywhere,* and you give me the yell, I'll yell back!" My poor wife! Little by little, kids embraced this convention as an open invitation to come talk to me, no matter where we were: football games, movie theaters, shopping malls, even just driving down the street with the windows down. Literally everywhere we went, I'd hear a kid yell out, "What's up, Pastor Scott?!" Many times, they'd see me before I saw them. I'd hear the yell, and I'd start darting my head around, looking for the child.

Always smiling, often shy faces would greet me every time. I'd often point right at them as I boomed back: "What's up, LifeKID?!" Sometimes deep, sometimes high, sometimes cartoony. Today, I can't go many places without hearing those words and turning to see a precious little boy or girl awaiting that familiar response from me, expecting it. What a blessing!

You answered the call. You decided this is who you are. Now you have to find ways to connect with the kids, *your kids*. Maybe it's a catchphrase for you, too. Or maybe it's a secret handshake. Maybe a special word or code. Whatever it is, start today. Ask God to reveal something that will not only help you break the ice, but that will actually bind your kids' hearts to you in love. Be crazy! Have fun! Scream across a mall. Who are you trying to impress, anyway? Connect with your kids!

—**Scott**

77

Wired Parents = Wired Partnership!

The parents in your ministry are wired. At the time of this writing, the latest Harris Interactive poll shows that 77 percent of U.S. adults are now online and 70 percent of adults are online at home.

The Internet gives you an opportunity to connect with parents. It can be a valuable ministry tool as you partner with them in their child's spiritual growth.

E-mail. E-mail can be a great way to partner with parents. You can send out a weekly or monthly e-mail newsletter to parents. It could contain information about upcoming lessons and events, parenting tips, lesson review questions, and current movie and music reviews. Use personal e-mails to communicate with and encourage parents.

Online surveys. Invite parents to take online surveys to give you feedback and ideas on how to make your ministry better. These could be done periodically after weekend services and after big events.

Parent website. A parent website could prove to be one of your best ways to connect with today's wired parents. If it's going to fly, then it's got to be a source of valuable help for them. You don't want to create a site that parents don't use. Try including articles and parenting tips for each stage of child development. Host a parent forum where they can discuss parenting challenges and ideas. Having movie and music reviews on your site is a valuable tool for parents as they make media choices for their families. (If you don't have the time to do the reviews yourself, then you can link to a great site like pluggedin.com.)

You could also post audio versions of previous lessons that parents can listen to, plus discussion questions from previous lessons. Include take-home papers for previous weeks in case they couldn't attend a service. And don't forget the online calendar and information about upcoming events and lessons.

Think of the possibilities: recommended list of Bibles and devotion books. Bios of the staff and contact information. Fun activities and ideas for family night. Local places to go for family fun. Available serving opportunities and how to get involved. Tips for keeping your kids safe online.

Consider wiring up your ministry. It's another great way to help today's wired parents become the spiritual leaders God has called them to be.

—**Dale**

78

What's in a Name?

What do you call your 2-year-old area? How about the people who serve in there every week? Have you ever thought about it? Does it matter? Yes. A thousand times: "Yes."

One of my favorite books is Tom Connellan's *Inside the Magic Kingdom: Seven Keys to Disney's Success.* This book has nothing and yet everything to do with ministry. Its principles and ideas have been instrumental in developing and growing our ministry, especially when it comes to names.

Names are powerful. Names mean things. You can influence results and shape vision with the names your ministry uses. Allow your names to share in the job of expressing your vision, your expectations, and your heart. People want to be a part of something bigger than themselves. Use names to help people not only see where they fit in your ministry, but to reinforce why their contribution is important.

Fix the vision, then name accordingly. We banished the word *volunteer.* Those who serve in our children's ministry are "cast" or "cast members." We assign roles instead of tasks. We renamed orientation to "casting call."

In every way that we could, we built an experience that supported this idea and reinforced it in name, expectation, and appearance. People caught on, and they bought in. They improved. The point was not that we simply changed the names of some things. We changed the culture.

Think like kids: What would they like to see? Here are some other examples in our ministry where we changed names to reinforce something vital to our success:

- *Not services, experiences.* We no longer use the word *services.* We say "experiences" instead, such as, "Come to the 10:30 experience." Why? Because that's what it is. A service is a funeral. We're offering people an opportunity to experience worship, to experience truth, to experience an invitation from Christ, and possibly to experience a total transformation by accepting the free gift of salvation. It's an "experience" not because of the name, but because of what it is.

- *Not classrooms, experiences.* What we do on the weekend is not simply an extension of the five-day school week...which, honestly, most kids don't like. These are not classrooms. They're experiences. There's not a single sign in our church that says "2-Year-Old Nursery" or "Fifth-Grade Classroom"...because that's not what we offer. How old is the word *nursery?* Is that what you *really* offer? Simply loving care for small children? No! We teach children of all ages the love of Jesus at a level appropriate to the age. We engage them with characters. We lead them to worship. In our ministry, we do this in experiences named "The Jungle" or "Under the Sea." These experiences are nothing like a classroom.

Use names to show people how valuable they are. It's so important, I want to return to our policy of no longer using the word *volunteer.* People think, *Hey, I'm just a volunteer. I can miss this week...*or, *They have lots of volunteers.* Most people care about titles. They feel a title represents how others perceive them. If the cast doesn't show up, the show can't go on. The cast members *are* the show.

God has called us to be servants. We are members of his body. When we invite people to serve, we're giving them an opportunity to respond to God's calling to *be* the church. Create an environment that brings these truths to life. Your ministry will respond.

Names mean things. You can go through your building and change the names of areas, meetings, and events, and that may begin to change things. But that will only work if the name truly represents something much bigger, much more real. If the name paints a true word picture of what you're trying to accomplish, what you're doing, then it has power—power to brand, to intrigue, to inspire, to empower.

Names matter.

—Scott

79

It's Not Nice to Point!

"Always remember, the magic begins with *you*."

—Be Our Guest, Perfecting the Art of Customer Service
by Disney Editions

How you treat the guests who walk in the doors of your church each week will directly affect your growth. Here are some simple, but strategic, ways to meet and even exceed guests' expectations.

Greet people...don't walk past them. Greet every person you come in contact with. Greet them with "Good morning" or "Welcome" or "Great to see you." You can tell when someone needs help. Don't walk past him or her. Go to the person immediately and ask, "Do you need some help?" or "May I help you?"

Smile...smile...smile! Always smile. A smile communicates joy... energy...love.

Look at people...not past them. Have you ever been talking to someone and you could tell the person really wasn't listening to you? He or she was look-ing over your shoulder or the look in the person's eyes said he or she wanted to make a quick getaway? I'm sure we've all been on both sides of that scenario. Look people in the eyes when you greet them. Stop and show genuine interest in them. Make them feel like the most important person in the world.

Say "I'm not sure, but I'll be glad to find out" instead of "I don't know." Isn't it frustrating when you ask someone a question and he or she just says, "I don't know!" You want to yell out, "Well, can you do something to find out instead of just standing there? I would appreciate it!" Never let the people in your church experience that frustration. If you don't know the answer, then go find it.

Walk...don't point. We live by this at our church. We walk people to where they need to go instead of pointing them toward it. This silently speaks volumes to the people who ask you for help.

Don't make them wait. Some people hide it better than others…but just about everyone hates a wait. Have enough check-in areas so the lines don't back up too far. Work hard at making check-in and pick-up lines move quickly. Have greeters that keep lines moving and flowing smoothly.

If people do have to wait for a short time, then engage them. The security lines at the Las Vegas airport are often backed up. I'm not quite sure why…there are only over 38 million guests in the city every year. Anyway, while you are waiting in those long security lines, they have strategically placed plasma TVs that play funny videos about going through security. It helps relieve the tension of the wait. We followed their cue and installed plasmas near our check-in areas. Now families can watch videos about upcoming events, lesson series, and activities during their short wait in line.

When people are waiting in line, it is also a great time to connect with them. Walk up and down the line greeting kids and families. Your greeting and interest in them can turn the wait into a pleasant experience.

Put people before rules. Rules are necessary, but when it comes to ministry, they should be flexible…not hard and unbending. We have rules, but if a rule stands in the way of someone having a great experience, then we will put the person before the rule. Here's an example. We close our room environments 20 minutes after the service has begun. If it's the last service of the day and a brand-new family walks in after the 20 minutes, then we are going to let them in the room. Being cordial to the new family will trump the rule. Always choose people over rules. (The only rules that we have no flex in are safety and security rules. There are no exceptions when it comes to following rules we have put in place to protect the children.)

Always be polite. No matter how silly the question may seem or how rude the person may be, always be courteous and polite. People can get frustrated when they are in a new place and are not sure what to do. Keep a kind and gentle spirit, no matter the situation or how they are acting.

A fellow staff member was telling me about a friend who works as a tech support guy for a computer company. A lady called and said she could not get her computer to come on. He walked her through many steps but she still couldn't get the computer to come on. He finally asked her to make sure it was plugged in. She responded that she couldn't check to see if it was plugged in because it was dark. He told her to turn the lights on. She said she couldn't because the power was off in the entire house! The tech guy was so frustrated after spending a long time with her that he told her to pack up the computer and send it back with a note that said "I am too stupid to operate a computer!" It's a true funny story, but it wasn't a good move on the part of the tech guy. The lady probably won't buy again from the company because of his remark. Always be polite…no matter what!

Roll out the red carpet for guests and attendees this week through your actions, words, and demeanor! But beware! It could lead to space issues because of all the people wanting to come to your church! And that's a good problem to have!

—Dale

When the Idea Becomes the Institution

I was speaking to a friend recently, sharing some recent significant changes in my life. This friend is a well-known figure in the American evangelical church, a noted speaker and author and respected minister of the gospel. He said something to me that shook me deeply. He said that as he looks around the large ministries in America, he continues to see examples of where an idea has transformed into an institution. It made me sad. Really sad.

Don't forget where you came from. It makes me think of Walt Disney, one of my heroes. This man had more passion and vision as a young man than most people will see in a lifetime. He risked everything for his dream. He loved people and wanted to make everyone smile, dreaming of "the happiest place on earth." Disney spent his entire life pursuing something people said could never happen. Today, entire denominations boycott his corporation and anything to do with it. Today, his dream has become a corporate conglomerate. Disney properties are still amazing places to visit. But I wonder—is Disney today really what Walt originally dreamed of, what he desired it to be?

The big "C" word. You know what it is: Change. Every organization experiences it. It's inevitable. It has to occur for success to continue. So why fight it, right? Wrong.

God has blessed each of us to share in his plan to reach the lost. To point children toward a loving Savior early in their lives. To partner with parents in equipping their children with the tools necessary to not only survive but to actually be salt and light to a dark, bleak world. We've been given a task, a vision, a dream to carry out. It's true that change is required for growth and relevance. But we have to be careful not to sacrifice that which called us in the first place. In scriptural terms, we can't forsake our first love.

Recognize the signs. Here are a few potential signs that may indicate you're starting to lose what made your ministry special in the first place:

- *Criticism.* If you catch yourself or those around you criticizing other ministries, pastors, or organizations—be cautious. Pride is waiting at the door.

- *Growth obsession.* When growth becomes the goal regardless of the cost—be cautious. Every ministry that's dying today was "on top" once.

- *Compromise.* When you compromise, and especially when you can justify it—be cautious. A single compromise today starts a slippery slope to a lifestyle of compromise tomorrow.

- *Rating yourself.* If you find yourself comparing your ministry to others—be cautious. If you need a measuring stick, look to Christ. He didn't have a big office, three assistants, or a big salary.

- *Over-hunger.* When enough is never enough—be cautious. Never allow your ministry to become bigger than what obedience asks of you.

- *Hurt people.* When casualties become a "necessary evil"—be cautious. Many times you're leaving more on the battlefield than you know. God's in the business of restoring people to himself, not wrecking them.

Keep the change. Change happens. There's no getting around it. But change can be managed, and just because it's change doesn't mean it's good. I pray that each of us will retain the vision God called us to. One day, we each want to hear him say, "Welcome, my good and faithful servant. Now enter into your reward."

—**Scott**

It's Gotta Be in Your DNA!

If you're going to raise up a great team of volunteers, serving has to be part of your church's DNA. It has to be a vital part of your core values. If there is an overall culture of service in the church, it puts you light years ahead as a children's minister striving to build a volunteer team.

At Central our spiritual growth strategy involves moving people through four simple steps. We want people to...

- **Plug In** to God and others at weekend services.
- **Charge Up** to become like Christ in small-group gatherings and First Wednesday.
- **Live Out** your faith by serving at Central and in our community.
- **Pass On** your faith to others.

Notice that one of the key steps is moving people into serving. It is a vital part of our strategy.

Here are some practical ways to see serving become a part of *your* church's DNA.

Teach about serving in your new members class. New members should be taught the importance of serving. Teach them that every member is a minister. Every member is expected to find a place of service.

At the class, provide a list of serving opportunities. Ask new members to indicate areas of interest. Pass on the information to your staff members, and have them connect with new members. I have found this method to be invaluable. There have been times I have enlisted 20 to 30 new children's ministry volunteers from one new members class.

Some churches have a waiting period before new members can serve. Use wisdom for when and where you place new members in service positions. See Idea 47 about appropriate steps in screening volunteers.

Ask people for a one-time service commitment—for times you most need help. Identify key times during your ministry year when you can ask people for a one-time service commitment. For us, Easter and Christmas services are when we have opportunities for lots of extra volunteers. During the weeks leading up to these two weekends, we purposefully ask people to sign up for a one-time commitment. Jud, our senior pastor, will talk about serving in the adult service, and we ask people to sign up right then. Their names are then passed on to the appropriate staff members, who plug them in.

Pair your one-time servers with key volunteers. Ask the key volunteers to share with them the joy and spiritual growth they receive from serving. Also, pairing them with key volunteers resolves any safety issues.

Have churchwide service campaigns during the year. Each year we do one or more churchwide pushes for people to serve. This is separate from the one-time service emphasis mentioned above. Have a different theme for each service campaign, and share stories of people who are currently serving and the difference it is making in their lives.

Present serving as an opportunity to live out your faith and make a difference. Don't present it as a "need." Show people the blessings and joy they can receive from serving.

Honor those who serve. Create a hospitality room for those who serve. Stock it with food, snacks, drinks, water, and occasional special goodies. Make the room comfortable with tables, chairs, and couches. Make it a place where volunteers can go to relax and hang out together before or after they serve. This will show that you value them and offer them a place to build community.

Honor a team of volunteers at least once a month in a worship service. Have them stand in the audience, and have the congregation cheer for them. This shows that you highly value those who serve.

—Dale

It cracks me up when I turn on the TV and see celebrities crying about their loss of privacy and the intrusions they have to endure. Not because I don't believe them, but because, well…it comes with the territory. If you want millions of people to pay nine dollars a ticket to go to a theater and see you save the world, I guess you have to give up the right to go to the mall without makeup and not get your picture taken.

In ministry, to a much smaller degree, you have to give up certain things, too. My pastor and I have had many conversations about the public demands of being in ministry, especially as a church begins to grow. The demands are real and, to be honest, difficult at times. But, just as it is for Hollywood, in our own little way, it's all part of the gig. As you serve the Lord, keep the following truths in mind:

Even if you haven't changed, everybody else is different. People will relate to you differently than before you were in ministry. You're no longer just a guy or a gal—you're a *minister*.

You're more than you are. People will hold you to a different standard now. Simply because you work at a church, people will expect more of you than they do of the person sitting next to them in a pew. They'll expect more of you than they do of themselves.

Sometimes you wanna go…where *nobody* knows your name. People will feel as if they know you. As you pour into people's lives, they will connect with you on a very personal level.

You are being watched. Whether you know it or not, people may recognize you, regardless of whether you know or recognize them. (Always use your napkin and your table manners.)

So, what do you do with this recognition or attention? How can you use this reality as a positive in your life and in your ministry? Here are a few ideas.

- *Accept it.* We have been given the privilege of influencing the lives of others. Responsibility comes with the privilege of influence.

- *Prepare your family.* So many times, my family is more affected by my recognition than I am. A church family will stop me as my family is walking out of a restaurant. My family will stand patiently waiting for me in the parking lot. People will walk up in the middle of a meal or a family activity, just wanting to say hi, even at a time when my family really needs my attention.

- *Set boundaries.* There are appropriate ways to defer a conversation without being rude. Generally, people will be understanding. Simply be cordial, with a wave or a brief greeting. Then move on.

- *Be above reproach.* We all bear the name of Christ. All our lives are supposed to be examples of our Savior to the world, whether we're employed by ministry or not. As we accept the additional layer of scrutiny that ministry brings, we must be extra careful where we go, what we say, how we act, what we drink, and so much more, so that we don't cause others to stumble.

- *Be thankful.* What an amazing opportunity ministry is! Understand that this is a gift, and you can and should use it to bless others and, most of all, to bring glory to God.

If celebrities can endure recognition for money and fame, certainly we can embrace it for eternal life change!

—**Scott**

Burnout Blues!

Sunday always returns. It never stops coming at you. Fifty-two weeks a year it stares you in the face. We like to call it "The Relentless Return of the Sabbath." Sunday is game day for children's ministry, and you've always got to be ready.

Unless you have a strategic plan, the relentless return of the Sabbath can have your volunteers singing the burnout blues. We jokingly say that church choirs are full of AWOL children's workers.

Here are some ways to help your volunteers avoid the burnout blues.

Place them where they are gifted. Nothing leads to burnout faster than people trying to serve where they are not gifted. Serving will quickly become a dread which will lead to them dropping out. Take time up front to help volunteers find their gift mix, and place them in a position that is a good fit for them.

Provide proper training. When people are thrown into a ministry position without training or a mentor, it can lead to a quick burnout. Provide new volunteers training and hands-on experience with a seasoned volunteer. I know you need that position filled now, but take the long look and empower that volunteer to serve for the long haul by providing him or her with proper training and a mentor.

Set a definite time period to serve. Many people think if they serve in children's ministry they will be tossed in a classroom, the door will be locked behind them, and they'll never be allowed out again. Ask people to serve for a specific time frame. We ask our volunteers to serve for one year. At the end of each ministry year, we ask if they would like to serve for another year. Some feel called to serve in other areas at the end of the year, but most come back.

Teach them to serve from the overflow. Burnout occurs when people are trying to serve from an empty spiritual tank. Teach people to fill their spiritual tanks and serve from the overflow of what God is doing in their lives. Teach your volunteers to keep their spiritual tanks overflowing by...

- daily prayer,

- daily confession of sin,

- daily Bible reading (give them a plan),

- being a part of an adult small group or Bible class (make sure they're doing life with adults and not just kids), and

- attending worship each week.

Provide a weekly devotion. Each week we send out an e-mail called "Team Notes." It contains not only upcoming information and lessons, but also a devotion volunteers can read. Volunteers constantly tell us that the devotions help them.

Ask them to serve in only one area. Every church has a few. They walk around with an S on their shirts. They are super volunteers and are so committed that they serve in several ministries simultaneously. The problem is that after awhile, the S falls off their shirts and they aren't serving anywhere. They over-commit and burn out. Encourage your volunteers not to serve in multiple areas.

Make preparation easy for them. When volunteers have to spend hours and hours each week preparing their lessons, it can lead to burnout. People are busier than ever before. Make preparing for Sunday easy. A well-written curriculum shouldn't take a teacher more than 30 minutes of preparation each week. We work hard at this. We use curriculum that our volunteers can read over three times and be ready to go. And when they walk in, all their supplies are ready and waiting for them.

Give them time off. When volunteers feel like they can't take a Sunday off, it can lead to burnout. Volunteers should be able to take a Sunday off when needed. We ask our volunteers to be here at least 85 percent of the time during the school year. That's 34 out of 40 weeks, meaning they can take off six weeks if needed. Build a strong enough team so when people are gone, your ministry doesn't miss a beat.

Consider canceling elementary children's services and activities on major holiday weekends. An example is Christmas weekend. Have your elementary kids attend worship with their parents on this weekend. This will give your volunteers a refreshing break during the holidays. During the summer, adjust your programming so volunteers can take off the whole summer if they'd like.

Have them serve in community. Serving alone can lead to burnout, but serving with a community of friends can be energizing. When you see volunteers developing close friendships, it's a great sign of team health. They will be there to encourage one another when someone gets weary.

God, give us people who refuse to sing the burnout blues!

—**Dale**

Who Are We?

One of my greatest privileges is being a father to my three sons—Dustin, Dillon, and Braden. Dustin and Dillon both live out of state now, but my little buddy Braden is still at home. For several years, Braden has played football in a city league. His team this year was the Packers. They had a great season, finishing third in the league for their age bracket. We learned a lot, made some great friends, and had a ton of fun. The best part was probably that the boys were led by a Christian coach. He had wrestled competitively in college, and he taught the boys how to both win and lose with character, how to have each other's backs, and how to play as a team, "as unto the Lord." It was a great year.

Know who you are. One team we played in the regular season was the Jets. These guys were huge and intimidating. And really good. We faced them again in the semifinals, when our team was much better prepared to play them. This team had one tradition in particular that really stood out to me. At regular intervals before, during, and after every game, one player or coach would call out, "WHO ARE WE?!" The entire team would respond (loudly), "JETS!" They'd repeat this back-and-forth chant four or five times, growing louder each time. It impressed us. It intimidated us. Perhaps most important of all, it unified *them*.

I remember thinking, *How great would that be, if we as believers—or even as children's ministers—adopted that same practice?* We'd proudly exclaim as a team, "WE LOVE GOD! WE LOVE KIDS! WE'RE ALL HIS!" Do you know who you are? Do you understand how important it is to not only know who you are, but to embrace it and share it with others?

Live who you are. If your church doesn't have stated values—a mission statement, a list of core values, or some written, guiding ideas like those— talk to your senior pastor about it. If your team and church body don't know who they are, they won't be willing to give their all to the church's vision. If you *do* have value statements established, incorporate them into your daily decisions, your team interactions, and your volunteer training sessions. As a unified team with a common language and common goals, you'll be able to accomplish more, and you'll experience greater unity.

Seek the Lord for his purpose, and seek direction from your leadership. Then boldly proclaim your mission, purpose, action steps, goals, values, and more! Together, with one voice, prepare your team to answer the call:
"WHO ARE WE?"

—Scott

I hate to break the news to you, but if you are reading this and you are out of college, then kids consider you an "old fogy." I know it hurts…but it's true. I turned 40 this past year, and most kids consider me ancient.

Don't get me wrong. You can still make a huge impact on kids no matter how "old" you are. But I believe the people who have the most potential to impact kids haven't even received their college degrees yet.

Who are they? Students. Students in junior high, high school, and college are positioned to influence kids even more than adults. Kids look up to students as their role models and heroes. It's who they want to be like. Companies such as Disney and Nickelodeon know this and fill their programming with students. Highly successful movies such as *High School Musical* are extremely popular with children. Look who is starring in the show…high school kids.

Each week we have dozens and dozens of students who serve in our children's ministry. Some of our best leaders are students. God is working in and through their lives in an incredible way. Here are some things we've learned when it comes to involving students in serving.

Make your children's ministry a place where students want to serve. Intentionally enlist students to serve. Teach them the importance of serving. Here are few ideas:

- *Plant seeds of service in your preteens.* As they are leaving your children's ministry, have them sign up to start serving as a junior high student.

- *Get students to enlist other students.* It's peer pressure the positive way!

- *Partner with the student pastor to create a student serving team.* This is key. The student pastor can help you enlist more students to serve than you could on your own.

- *Give them their own identity.* Have shirts designed for your student serving team. Make being part of the student serving team a big deal!

Have a process in place for students who want to join the team. We basically follow the same process for students as we do for adults who want to serve. Here are the steps:

- *Student fills out an interest card.*
- *Student observes in the environment.*
- *One-on-one interview is done.* We normally ask the student to have a parent attend this meeting. We want to make sure the parent understands and is supportive of the commitment the student is making.
- *Student fills out a serving application.* This includes a parental permission form if the student is under 18.
- *Student attends orientation.*
- *Student begins serving.* Student is placed with a seasoned volunteer. Training and hands-on experience is provided.

Age breakdown. We normally follow this age guideline for students serving, but it can vary based on the maturity of the students:

- *Grades 6-8 can serve in the preschool through third-grade environments.*
- *Grades 9-college can serve in the preschool through fifth-grade environments.*

Make sure students stay involved in their own ministry. This is important. We require students to be involved in their own student ministry if they are going to serve in children's ministry. If you're not careful, children's ministry can become a hiding place for students who can't seem to find their fit in their own age-appropriate ministry. Partner with the student pastor to keep students who are serving in children's ministry connected to their own ministry as well.

Hold them accountable. When you involve students in serving in children's ministry, you have to remember they are still just big kids. They will act silly, do goofy stuff, and make mistakes. That's OK. You want the energy and excitement of their youthfulness in the room. But you also want to make sure they are following the guidelines you have in place. You want to create a fun but controlled environment for students to serve in. The energy and passion of youth must be guided by the wisdom and experience of maturity. When you bring the two together, it can be dynamic!

Remember that students grow up. Many of the best adult volunteers I've ever met first started serving when they were students. They have years of experience as a result. When you enlist students to serve, you are laying a volunteer foundation for years to come.

When I was 16, my student pastor approached me about serving in children's ministry. I agreed, and 24 years later I'm still serving in children's ministry. God used my high school service to light a fire in my soul for children's ministry that still burns today.

There are lots of other students who are just like I was. They are just waiting to be asked to join your team. They're full of energy, potential, and dreams. Release them into your children's ministry, and watch them make a "Sweet 16" impact!

—**Dale**

Have you ever heard the phrase "Pick your battles"? Do you think that's wise? And how do you know when to keep fighting and when to let an issue go? Here's how I learned.

In the early stages of our ministry, we totally remodeled our children's space. One key component was to be an amazing, talking, singing, animatronic tree, situated in the middle of the main campus thoroughfare. Using music and conversation, the tree would intrigue children, be an epicenter where they would want to gather. Then the tree would share simple, short stories from God's Word with kids and their families.

Plans were humming. Then one day I was updating our leadership in a meeting. Suddenly, as I related our vision, great opposition surfaced. "The tree should be old and wise." "The tree should be male instead." "I don't like the name." Everyone seemed to have an opinion. I was confused, bewildered. I never saw this coming.

Have you ever been there? One minute you're sure of the vision and inspiration you received from God. Then suddenly you find yourself having to defend that vision to others. So what do you do? I learned some valuable truths which have stayed with me ever since.

Believe and ask. Matthew 21:22 says simply that if you believe, you will receive whatever you ask for in prayer. God answers when we ask. His Word promises it. Standing on this passage, our team diligently prayed, asking God to reveal his plan to us. He did.

Prepare. Then prepare some more. Be well-prepared *before* it's time to share your vision with others. Leaders are looking for conviction. If you don't prepare, your scattered thoughts are likely to misrepresent your passion and your vision.

Submit to authority. Always submit to your God-given authorities. There is no allowance for rebellion in Scripture. God never honors it. God clearly places those in authority over us, and his policies regarding how we are to respect them, respond to them, and pray for them are also clear. Hold up your end in a conflict, but respect their input as leaders.

Answer for yourself: Did God speak? If he did, then why worry? Believe in what God told you. When you know God has spoken, hold tight and don't compromise in what he's instructed you to do. Also, understand that there are many ways to end up where you need to be. Sometimes you may have to creatively navigate through an issue to end up where you're going. Trust in the Lord to ultimately provide the way to fulfill his will.

Accept risk. Many times, other leaders are looking for resolve in you, a passion for what you bring to the table. This goes hand in hand with both preparation and submission to authority. That's where your confidence, your resolve, and your willingness to accept risk come from.

So, back to that meeting about the tree. It ended in total disagreement, but I stood my ground. Others stood theirs. I was frustrated and confused. My direct supervisor encouraged me, "Hold on. Don't give up. Give God a chance to work things out." So I prayed: *If I missed it, please reveal it so I can be corrected. But if I heard clearly, please fulfill your Word.* As I trusted in God and placed the situation back in his hands, he revealed his will.

Early the next morning, my phone rang. My boss had been doing his daily devotional. God had given him a passage for that day that not only confirmed our vision, but solidified the same thing in his heart as well. Later that morning, as we met with the other leaders, we simply shared this revelation. Immediately, unanimously, everyone agreed that God had spoken. It was never discussed again. God's will prevailed.

—**Scott**

87

Preteen Ministry That Rocks!

Many children's ministries tend to reach more younger-elementary children than upper-elementary kids. This is often reflected in attendance patterns. Take a hard look at your attendance for each grade. Do you see a downhill pattern from first- to fifth- or sixth-grade?

There can be many factors involved. The older kids get busier, their parents may divorce so they can only come every other week, or in some cases, perhaps we are no longer relevant to their needs. Perhaps we are not engaging them, building relationships with them, and connecting with them.

Here are some key elements of a preteen ministry that rocks.

Identity. Preteens often seem like they're floating in a mysterious zone that lies somewhere between elementary school and junior high. One minute they'll be downloading the latest hits onto their iPods while IM'ing their friends, and the next minute they're playing LEGOS with their siblings. They are "too cool" for "little kid" stuff, but nervous about entering junior high ministry. A preteen ministry can give them the identity they need as they transition between two worlds.

IDEAS

- Give your preteen ministry a unique name, look, and logo.

- Give preteens their own environment (room). Ask for their insight and ideas as you decorate. Pick a theme that reflects their culture.

- Consider the age grading of your local school when determining which grades will be a part of your preteen ministry.

Teaching. Children haven't changed, but childhood has. Today's preteens increasingly face issues that their parents didn't face until they were older teens. Thirteen is the new 16. Know the issues your preteens are facing. What do they need to know? Teaching should be designed to meet the needs of preteens head-on.

- Teach topical series on subjects such as peer pressure, friendship, and self-esteem.

- Teaching should prompt preteens to ask the tough questions they need to struggle through. "Why is the Bible true?" "Were we created or did we evolve?" "Why is Jesus the only way to heaven?"

- Make teaching fun, interactive, and participatory. Preteens don't want to be lectured…they want to be a part of the learning experience.

Programming. Lean heavily toward the junior high side when programming for preteens. Music, videos, lessons, skits, games, and other parts of programming should reflect a junior high look and feel.

IDEAS

- Make the oldest boy in the room your programming target. If he thinks it's "cool," then you will hit every preteen in the room.

- Programming should be energetic, wacky, and fun. Preteens love messy games, loud music, and crazy skits.

Relationships. The number-one element of a preteen ministry that rocks is a great volunteer team of leaders. Leaders who build relationships with preteens and invest their lives in them. Show me a rockin' preteen ministry, and I'll show you a group of rockin' preteen leaders!

IDEAS

- Provide specialized training for your preteen leaders. Help them know and understand the unique needs of today's preteens.

- Small groups are a great way to help your leaders build relationships with preteens. Form small groups of six to eight preteens per leader. Keep the same kids and leaders together each week so they can build relationships.

- Spiritually mature high school kids make good leaders for preteens. Many times high school kids are heroes to preteens.

Partnership. An effective preteen ministry partners with parents. As preteens move into and go through puberty…well, you know what happens. Parents are looking for answers to help them guide their quickly changing kids. Come alongside parents and give them tools, resources, and encouragement.

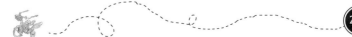

- Have regular focus groups with parents of preteens. This will give you insight and information on how to better partner with them.
- Give parents the lesson questions and activities so they can talk with their kids about what was covered at church.
- Provide parenting tips and resources that target the preteen years.

Events. Have events just for your preteens. They love things such as sleepovers, trips, retreats, and outings.

- Ask your small-group leaders to go to these events. This can be a great time for them to build relationships outside of the weekend service.
- Encourage your preteens to invite their unchurched friends to events.
- Have a summer camp just for preteens.

Serving. Preteens are eager to serve. It's definitely time to help them put feet to their faith. Get them involved in serving both inside and outside the church.

- Let preteens serve in the preschool and lower elementary areas. Use wisdom in knowing which service opportunities to place them in.
- Get preteens involved in serving in their own age-level ministry.
- Help preteens do group service projects in the community.
- Take preteens on short-term mission projects.

Big business marketers know the importance of reaching out to preteens, and they spend billions of dollars each year trying to gain their attention. For them, it's about cashing in on preteen buying power and building brand loyalty at a young age.

We must be just as diligent and strategic as we reach out to preteens. We must grab their attention so we can help them become loyal Christ-followers. God wants to work in their lives in a major way during this critical life stage. For many of them, it will be the crossroads where they decide which direction to go. Let's be there…pointing them toward God!

—Dale

Leadership had approved us to make a new hire. We met a candidate in the interview process who seemed the perfect fit. We made the offer. The person accepted. It was all downhill from there...

It became immediately clear, and I mean within days, that we had made a mistake. Now, this person was not a bad person but was clearly a bad fit. It became very painful. What were we supposed to do? We had begged leadership for this hire. We were so confident this was the right person. We asked this person to redirect their whole life to take this job.

Wow! That was a mistake.

Have you ever made a mistake that really caught you off guard? Boy, I have! Actually, I've made tons of them. That one hiring mistake in particular taught me some lessons that I'll never forget.

You may have the privilege of having paid staff, or your team may be completely volunteer. Regardless, you're in the business of gathering people to help in your ministry, right? The right people make all the difference in the world. Unfortunately, so do the wrong ones.

Through the counsel of my boss—one of the best in this area—and through the pain of the experience, we determined several criteria that helped us bring people in...and let them go, if necessary.

Don't rely too much on first impressions. People can often project whoever they want to be in an interview process. It takes more than a few conversations to see the real person inside. In the same way, some people, people who will one day become superstar team members, may interview terribly. A first impression is never the best indicator for a successful hiring.

Look at the whole person. Our leadership assembled an elaborate series of tests that applicants must go through to give us a more balanced picture of the whole person. These tests included a Myers-Briggs personality test

(MBTI), several general skills tests, a spiritual gifts test, an EQ-I (emotional intelligence) test, and a strategic line of questioning for us to use during interviews.

Involve different perspectives on your interview team. Many times, based on your own biases, you may perceive an applicant totally different from the way someone else on your team does. Allow your interview team to represent a cross-section of your overall team. Having different genders, different personality types, and different learning skills represented will serve you well in your post-interview download.

Realize that you will make mistakes. In our ministry, every position begins with a mandatory 90-day probationary period, during which time the employee can be released for any reason, without any recourse. Harsh? Maybe. Necessary? Absolutely. (Some leadership positions have a one-year period.)

Know the position you're hiring for. Never try to build a position around a person, as tempting as that may be. Always look at your organization, see the greatest needs, and then hire according to those needs.

Admit it when you make a mistake...as quickly as possible. It's no fun to tell leadership you were wrong. It's always rough sailing letting someone go from your team, paid or non-paid, whether a new hire or a veteran. It's no fun to start the whole hiring process again. But none of these pains compares to the long-term damage incurred from placing or allowing the wrong person on your team to remain in the wrong role. Suck it up. Do what has to be done. Ultimately, it's best for everyone.

Remember the person's feelings. Most applicants see ministry as a step of obedience to God. Understanding this, we must be very cautious in the process of letting a person go. It's extremely difficult for a person who is discharged not to take it personally, not to let it affect his or her feelings about the church and church leadership. Worse, the person may even begin to question his or her ability to hear clearly from God. Remember how big this is to the person.

Your team of paid staff or volunteers is your greatest asset. Not having the right people will kill you. Having the right people will allow you to accomplish impossible things. Be strategic. Be diligent in the appointment process. Pray for guidance and peace. Take advantage of the many personnel tools available on the market today. Do your best to hire the right people.

Correct your mistakes quickly…and learn from them. Do everything you can to avoid having to say…

"Wow! That was a mistake."

—**Scott**

At Your Service!

> "For even the Son of Man came not to be served but to serve others and to give his life as a ransom for many."
>
> —Mark 10:45

A few years ago, our class of fifth-grade girls decided they wanted to do a service project. Pam, their teacher, shared an article with the girls that she had recently read in Reader's Digest. The article was about a girl named Sarah who was paralyzed. She was confined to a wheelchair but had remarkable talents. She couldn't talk, but wrote stories by using a computer that she controlled by breathing through a special tube. The girls decided to adopt Sarah as their service project and contacted her mother. They found out her biggest need was a special feeding machine that would enable her to feed herself. Her family was underprivileged and could not afford the machine. It would cost over $3,000.

The girls decided to go for it. They washed cars, sold cookies, and did other projects to raise the money. Through lots of hard work, they soon had enough money to buy the machine. The easy thing would have been to ship the machine to Sarah. But the girls felt they should deliver it to her in person. They raised extra money and rented a bus. We drove them eight hours one way to deliver the feeding machine to Sarah. I will never forget the night they met her and gave her the machine. They sang to her, shared poems they had written for her, told her of God's love, and ministered to her. Sarah spoke to them through a computer-generated voice that was controlled by the breathing tube. There wasn't a dry eye in the room as Sarah thanked them for the machine.

Teach the importance of serving. On a regular basis, intentionally teach about serving and giving of yourself to others. Recently we had a lesson about giving to others. We gave every child a bag of candy with a card in it that explained the gospel. We told the kids the candy was not for them. Each child was to give it to an unchurched friend that week as a gift. It wasn't easy for kids to give away the candy, but it provided a great teaching experience about serving others.

Regularly challenge kids to live out their faith by serving others. Give them small, practical ways they can serve others during the week. The next week, check in to see how kids followed through.

Provide local group service projects. Take groups of kids to clean up parks, rake a widow's yard, pass out free bottled water, and so on. Always make sure you have a proper adult-to-child ratio and that the service area is a safe environment for the kids.

Spend time in prayer with the kids before you go. Later spend time downloading with the kids after the service project. Let them share how it felt, what it meant to them, and how it helped them grow spiritually.

Provide opportunities for families to serve together. When kids serve with their parents, I believe it doubles the impact it has on their lives. Two years ago, we put together a plan for our church families to bring Christmas to needy families in our area. Our church families could purchase a Christmas tree, gifts, and a meal and then personally deliver it to the home of the needy family. We heard great reports of how this impacted kids and parents as they did this service project together.

Projects that take a big time-commitment, such as helping build a home for a needy family, are wonderful. But be sure you balance big projects with smaller projects so lots of families can get involved. Provide parents with a list of discussion questions to use with their kids after the project is finished. It will deepen the experience and help kids reflect further on the importance of serving others.

Provide kids opportunities to share their faith through serving. At one church, I taught the kids how to share their faith using the witness bracelet (colored beads). After they learned how to use the bracelet, we borrowed an ice-cream truck. We loaded the truck with ice-cream bars and hit the streets with that annoying music blaring away. As kids would gather around the truck, our kids would come out of the truck and give out the free ice cream. Our kids would then share their faith with them by using the witness brace-lets. It was awesome seeing our kids share the gospel with dozens of kids that summer.

Another time the kids attached gospel cards to bottles of cold water and we passed the water out at local ball fields on a hot summer day. The kids always got excited when we shared the gospel by serving others.

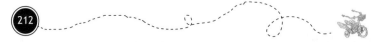

Provide opportunities that will open people's hearts to the gospel message as your kids learn the value of serving others *and* sharing their faith.

Lead kids and families on short-term mission projects. Let's face it. Lots of kids in America are spoiled. From the latest video games to their own cell phones to plasma TVs with hundreds of cable channels…they have it all. One of the best things they could ever experience would be a mission trip. A trip where they get dirty…sleep on a cot…can't get cell phone reception… work hard to serve others. It can be a life-changing experience and a spiritual growth catalyst.

If you choose this option, make the trip for upper-elementary/preteen kids. Encourage parents to go. Again, the impact can be doubled when parents are involved. And give kids opportunities to share what they experienced when you return. This will instill in other kids the desire to serve when they hear the experiences of the kids who went on the trip.

The Millennial Generation, as today's kids have been called, want to make the world a better place. They are goal-oriented and driven. They are ready to be committed to a cause. They are ready to serve…they're just waiting for our lead.

Let's raise up a generation of kids who are like Jesus…who would rather serve than be served. A generation like that can change the world!

—**Dale**

90

///////////////////////////

You Call This a Church?

///

An older elementary boy sauntered into our lobby for the first time one Easter Sunday and froze, slack-jawed. Looking around, he said, "You call this a *church?!*" A member of my team who was present when this happened couldn't wait to tell the rest of us. Why? Because we've done everything we can to make our church not look, feel, or sound like a church—at least not the way most people expect a church to be. That day, it worked.

The excitement, the music, and the amazing environments all combined to overwhelm his senses, catch him off guard. When he entered his experience, he was greeted by other kids his age, video game stations, and conversation stations. He probably had to raise his voice to be heard over the music videos running on four video screens. During the experiences, he was confronted by the truth of God's Word—that Jesus loved him. Everything was intentional, all wrapped up in a package he could relate to. A package that did not, in *his* mind, equal church.

Jesus wants us to seek the lost so he can save them. Our pastor says that we, the church, should do anything short of sin to reach the lost. Evangelism is one of our core values. It's the best one-word description of my pastor's vision. As the children's ministry component, we're committed to fulfilling that purpose in everything we do.

How are you planning to earn the right to be heard by a child? It doesn't have to be a cool environment (although that never hurts), but it had better be something strategic. How can you line up with the vision of your church and still reach today's kids?

Keep Jesus alive. Maybe you're thinking, "This guy is crazy" or "This is blasphemy! We will *never* do things in God's house to entice children to come." It's OK if you feel that way. I know a lot of people who do. But I promise you this: If you base your children's ministry on your preferences, on what's acceptable to *you,* then your children's ministry is in trouble. A few years ago, I was at the Children's Pastors' Conference in Dallas, seated at a table with eight other children's ministers I didn't know. The presenter onstage was showing a new product that his company was releasing. His presentation had loud music, guys dressed up in costumes, and all kinds of other craziness. I was mesmerized, and during his presentation, I determined that immediately following the session I was going to go find his booth.

I was astonished when an older gentleman at our table spoke up loudly, "That's ridiculous! I would *never* allow garbage like that in my ministry!" His remark both offended and saddened me. Somewhere in America, there are little kids whose parents have decided that they'll try that man's church this Sunday. These children will be taught and reached out to by the preferences of a man whose mind isn't open to new ideas. Since that day, I've thought many times about that man, wondering how his ministry is doing. Are kids finding the one, true, living Jesus there?

Do unto children as you'd have done unto you. Kids will absolutely not listen to you just because they're a captive audience. Don't believe me? Ask any school teacher.

You have to earn their attention, win their trust, engage their imaginations, entice their curiosity, and give them an experience they would choose to repeat again and again.

There's so much at stake. This generation *must* hear the gospel. They can listen to it on a podcast. Or watch it on their iPods. Or experience it on a website. Whatever the packaging, the contents are too precious, too vital, too transforming, not to be heard. I pray that every child who walks through our doors will freeze, overwhelmed, caught off guard, and say out loud (or at least think), "You call this a *church?!*"

—**Scott**

91

Digital Playground

"Kids' rooms are becoming kind of like mini-media centers."
—Ron Geraci, Nickelodeon's Senior VP of Audience Research

Kids love to play. That hasn't changed and never will. But what has changed is their playground. Today's kids are immersed in a digital playground. They are "wired" for play.

Eighty-six percent of young people have a computer at home. Seventy-four percent have a home Internet connection. The most common recreational activities young people engage in on the computer are playing games and communicating through instant messaging. The average amount of time kids spend on a computer each day (outside of schoolwork) has doubled in the last six years. On any given day, 73 percent of 8- to 10-year-old boys will play video games.

Kids also use technology to access one of their greatest loves…music. The Internet is used to listen to and download songs. Almost two-thirds of kids have a portable music device. iPods and MP3 players abound.

The typical child lives in a home that has 3.5 TVs. Dozens, if not hundreds, of channels are available at any time. Movies are available for instant purchase and viewing.

Cell phones used to be something adults bought for business purposes. Today, parents are buying them for their kids at younger and younger ages.

Kids are spending more time than ever in the digital playground. If you want to connect with today's kids, then you need to enter that playground. Use their digital toys as conduits to share God's truth. Here are some ways to do that.

Before implementing any of the following ideas, be sure to inform parents and obtain their permission.

E-mail. E-mail newsletters, devotions, and discussion questions. Create e-vites (church online invitations) that they can forward to invite their friends.

Internet. Give kids the addresses of websites that share the gospel, and challenge kids to send the links to their friends. (Eighty-eight percent of sites that kids visit come from friends' recommendations.)

Provide links to sites with online daily devotionals for kids. Have computers available in the classroom for kids to surf the Web before and after class, play games, research Bible topics, and do Bible lessons (with supervision).

Create a website. With parental approval, create a website for your children's ministry where kids can see pictures of past events, vote on which songs they'd like to sing next week, participate in online contests, answer lesson review questions, do online devotions, watch videos, and play games.

You could also create an online community for the kids in your ministry. Group Publishing's preteen curriculum called Grapple gives you easy tools to do this.

Media. Use clips from popular television shows and movies as lesson illustrations.

Studies show that a big reason kids like technology is because it helps them build friendships. Technology has enabled young people to have constant connectivity. Kids are longing to be known and feel valued. We can use technology to help them get connected to other Christ-followers. And most important, we can use it to help them get connected to the greatest friend of all…Jesus.

—**Dale**

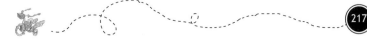

92

You Have to Be This Tall to Ride

Our church had just spent thousands of dollars in renovations. My team had prepared for months. We were ready. The big weekend was finally here! The grand opening! I was on top of the world. Then *she* showed up. I will (unfortunately) never forget one of the first weekends in our new space, when one mom pulled me aside. She was clearly upset. In less than three minutes, she identified what a dirty scoundrel I was, explained how I didn't understand anything about children, and revealed that she knew my dirty "secret": that I only cared about numbers. Where was this all coming from? She wanted her 5-year-old to be allowed to attend our elementary experience, Toon Town… designed for children ages 6 and up.

Get out the measuring stick. Have you ever seen that little boy at the amusement park? You know the one I mean. He's at the front of the line, standing on his tippy-toes, straining for his mohawk to…just…barely… brush…the bottom of the measuring stick held by the ride operator (who's rolling his eyes). Unfortunately for him, sometimes you just have to be "this tall" to ride. That's the rule.

Have you ever noticed that no matter how hard you try, you can't please everyone? Have you ever noticed that no matter how good something is, someone will still be unhappy? Have you ever noticed that when God is blessing what you're doing, someone inevitably arrives to steal your joy, to distract your focus, to bring you down? Me too! So how do we react? Through years of dealing with thousands of families, I've identified the following truths:

Be vigilant. The enemy is coming. Satan knows how to hurt you. In 2 Corinthians 2, Paul reminds us that we should not be outsmarted. Instead, we should be aware of the evil one's schemes. He strikes us where we're most vulnerable. Remember: People are not your enemy. Not parents. Not other people in ministry. You have one enemy. *One.* Watch for him.

Expect it: You can't please everyone. For every leadership decision you make, expect someone to be unhappy. With the differences in personalities, tastes, experiences—and even convictions—it's impossible to please everyone. Don't try. In Galatians 1:10, Paul reminds us: We're not striving to win man's approval, but God's.

Know two things: What's the rule? Why do we have it? What's the rule in question? Is it for the individual child's protection? Is it for the safety of the other children in the room? Is it a requirement of your insurance carrier? Know your rules, and know why you have them. Then when outside forces challenge your leadership, you can stand behind the rules with authority.

Stand your ground. Decide what matters. Then hold true to it. Commit. If it's valid, uphold it for everyone. But if you recognize that a rule is (or has become) unnecessary, don't carry on an unhealthy relationship with it. Move on. Change it for everyone. But in every case, be consistent.

Always speak the truth *in love*. Ephesians 4:15 instructs us to speak the truth in love. That's hard. It's hard to face conflict, especially because we can't control how others will react. But we're always responsible for how we act. God is love. We need to reflect that.

Carry on. Live your call. I've learned to read hate mail and not take it personally. I've learned that anything that was submitted "anonymously" was not worth my time. I've learned that people say things in the heat of the moment...and later regret those words. I've learned that it's easy to let one negative, off-the-cuff remark outweigh 100 encouraging, affirming words. I've learned that the issue is rarely with the child...but almost always with the adult. Even if someone blames you—even if someone's ready to "leave the church over it"—sometimes...

You just have to be this tall to ride.

—**Scott**

93

Leading Through Change

Change is not always easy. It moves us out of our comfort zone into uncertainty. It requires us to step out in faith. It means we are letting go of the past and reaching out in risk.

Our family experienced this when God called us to do ministry in Las Vegas. We had been at our previous church for over seven years. We were comfortable. We had a great group of kids and families that we were ministering to. We were surrounded by people who loved us. We had just built a new home. We were in the process of designing a new, multimillion dollar children's building.

And then God said, "It's time to let go. I want you to leave your comfort zone and go to Las Vegas to share my love with the kids and families there." It was a hard decision. It was a huge move for us…a big change. But we made the move, knowing the change was God's will.

If your children's ministry is going to be relevant in the days ahead, then you will have to be effective at leading it through change. Here are some insights that will help you do that:

Remember, change means opportunity for growth. Things that are growing are changing. My son Caleb was 21 inches when he was born. He is now taller than his mom and at age 13 is about to catch me. What caused the change? Growth! Change is what breaks us out of a rut. Change brings the potential to go to a new ministry level. Has your children's ministry reached a plateau or is it declining? Change can bring about the growth you need.

Hold the ministry with open hands. There are churches that are dying because they refuse to change. They hold on tightly to programs, methods, and traditions that are no longer effective. The death knell of "we've never done it that way before" is heard. The church gets emptier with each passing year, and a "we are the faithful, holy remnant that is holding on to the end" mentality is adopted. The old ways have become so sacred that God's message is not being communicated with relevance.

We must be willing to hold our ministries with open hands. The message is timeless and unchanging, but we must be willing to change our methods, programs, and philosophies when needed.

Create a culture of change. Teach people that change is good. Show them the necessity of shifting and adjusting to stay relevant. Honor the past, but teach your team not to worship it. Help them see that you can't live on past victories. Teach them to have the mind of Paul when he said in Philippians 3:13b-14, "Forgetting the past and looking forward to what lies ahead, I press on to reach the end of the race and receive the heavenly prize for which God, through Christ Jesus, is calling us."

Vision leads to change. When I first came to Central, I met with key volunteer leaders and shared a vision of what the children's ministry could be. They bought in because it was a big vision that would help us more effectively reach kids and families. It also meant making changes, but they realized the changes were necessary to help us fulfill the vision.

Effectively communicate change. The majority of people are open to change. They just want to know what's going on and give their input. Go the extra mile to communicate change and solicit people's ideas and insight.

For major changes, start your communication with two or three key leaders. Share with them why the change needs to happen, and get their input. Take their ideas and insight, and tweak your plan as needed.

Then go to a larger group of key leaders (10-15). Repeat the same process. Then go to an even larger group of key leaders (50-75). Repeat the process again. Keep going until you are ready to share the change with everyone. The numbers will obviously vary depending on the size of your team. The point is to start with a small communication circle and expand from there.

Realize that change can result in some fallout. Not everyone is going to be happy with change. The majority of people will come on board when you share the vision and let them have a part in the planning and implementation. A smaller percentage of people will need time to process the change. Walk patiently with them. Show grace and understanding. Keep casting the vision that's driving the change. They will probably come around in time. But a few people just can't accept change. They will leave. That's OK. It hurts, but you cannot let it stop you from fulfilling God's plan for your ministry.

Realize that change is all about timing. Sometimes change must be implemented swiftly. Other times it can be a slow process. Ask God for wisdom and understanding to discern the right timing. You want the right change with the right timing.

What will your children's ministry look like in five years? You shouldn't know the answer to that question right now. Your ministry boat is in a culture that is a rushing, roaring river, not a placid pond. You must be willing to shift, adjust, and change as needed to stay relevant. We can't know where the river will take us, but we can be ready to navigate through the changes that lie before us.

—**Dale**

94

You Probably Don't Have What It Takes

Since I've been in ministry, I've received the following call numerous times, typically with a young, energetic voice on the other end:

Caller: Is this Scott?

Scott: Yes.

Caller: Hi, Scott this is _____. I'm calling today on behalf of _____, a professional search firm.

I smile. It's a headhunter. Let the games begin...

Caller: Scott, I'm representing a large church in _____, and I was given your name as a possible prospect for a position we've been retained to fill.

Sometimes I stop them here, because I know where this is going. Other times I just let them go on, because...well, you'll see...

Scott: Great! What church?

Caller: Well, Scott, I'm not at liberty to disclose that at this time. But I was wondering, may I ask you a few questions?

Scott: Sure.

Caller: Great, thanks! How long have you been in ministry?

Scott: 1/3/5 year(s). *(This answer depended on when they called.)*

Caller: Oh, OK...Well, um, where were you before your present church?

Scott: I worked in the real estate industry.

Caller: Oh, OK...So this is your first church?

Scott: It's the first church where I've worked. Is that what you mean?

Caller: Sorry, yes. OK, um, where did you attend seminary or Bible college?

Scott: I didn't.

Caller: Um, where did you graduate from college?

Scott: I didn't.

Caller: All right. Well...I certainly appreciate your time. Have a nice day.

Scott: Thank you for calling.

At this point I lean back in my chair, smile, and think to myself, *You know, Scott, they're right. You're probably not qualified.*

The best success stories are the ones no one ever sees coming. Have you ever been told you can't do something that God said you can? My pastor, now the pastor of one of the largest churches in America, once sat before a board and was told that he didn't have what it took to lead a church.

God has used every experience of my life to prepare me for my role in children's ministry. From having Christian parents, to being raised in the church, to accepting Christ as my Savior early in life, to being a bed-wetter so I could relate to kids afraid to go to camp. Everything I'd ever done prepared me.

Through these phone calls, I'm convinced God was gently, teasingly reminding me of my incompetence and of the fact that he likes it that way. When I remember how unqualified I am, I'll rely more on him, his guidance, and his grace.

God rarely calls the equipped, but he always equips the called. God gave Moses a tongue to speak. He gave Peter the courage to stand before huge crowds and proclaim truth. He gave Stephen a resolve in his faith that would sustain him even unto death. He always provides whatever's needed to carry out his will.

God sees things we can't see. He created you with a specific purpose. And then he providentially placed you in this time and in this place, so he could use you to carry out his will.

Get out of your own way. You can do all things through Christ. You know the verse from Philippians. Do you live it? If God has called you, you can do it!

And you're not alone. Whether they admit it or not, people all around you have been told at least once that they don't have what it takes. Don't be intimidated. If God is with you, who can be against you?

Be thankful when God checks your pride. When someone scoffs at your qualifications, it's just another opportunity for you to acknowledge how much you need and rely upon the Good Shepherd to lead you and protect you.

I like how Paul says it in 2 Corinthians 12:10: "That's why I take pleasure in my weaknesses…For when I am weak, then I am strong."

So take heart. Follow God's voice, no matter what people say. Are we here to please them, or him? Forge ahead. Let them scoff. Keep going. Let them whisper that you don't have what it takes. Then go do your job. Do it with excellence. Do it with your whole heart, as unto the Lord.

Lose your life. And you just might find it.

—Scott

95

Turn on the Scoreboard!

Dallas Cowboys 27
Pittsburgh Steelers 17

—Scoreboard From Super Bowl XXX in Tempe, Arizona

I love the Dallas Cowboys! Always have…always will. When I first saw them play as a child, I knew they would be my team for life. Win or lose…I'm with them to the end. On a fall Sunday afternoon, you'll find me in front of the television cheering for them. Occasionally, I even get to watch them play in person. I've been known to jump up and down and yell like a crazy man when they score.

It's easy to know when the Cowboys have scored. The points go up as they cross the goal line, kick a field goal, or get a safety on the other team. But how do we know when we've "scored" in children's ministry? You have to be willing to turn on the scoreboard.

Turning on the children's ministry scoreboard can be exciting and scary at the same time. It means everyone will see when you score, but it will also reveal when you fall short of the goal line.

First…design a scoring system for the scoreboard. Decide for each event, activity, environment, or program what will put points on the board. It may be attendance, kids taking a spiritual step, kids grasping a spiritual truth, parents getting involved, or first-time guests present.

Second…power up the scoreboard. Everything you do should be powered by prayer. Points won't go on the board without prayer. Give it your very best, but depend on God to help you score points. Nothing of eternal value is accomplished without prayer.

Third…put points on the scoreboard. Come up with a strategic action plan for each program, event, activity, or environment. The strategic action plan should be made up of specific steps that move you down the field to score. Give team members ownership of the steps, and hold them accountable to complete them.

Fourth…have a post-game report based on the scoreboard. After the event, activity, or program, sit down and talk about how it went. What steps helped you put points on the board? What kept you from scoring? What can help you put more points on the board next year?

Fifth…use the scoreboard to track player stats. Scoreboards are often used to post player stats. Sit down with new team members and show them what the "scores" are for the volunteer positions they are accepting. This will give your team members clear goals and direction. Then meet with them periodically to help them measure their progress. Ask if there is anything you can do to help them continue moving forward. Give them a "pat on the back" for their contribution to the team. When one person scores…the whole team scores!

Sixth…celebrate the scoreboard! Don't forget to look up at the scoreboard regularly and celebrate the points with your team! Spike the ball and do some end-zone dances together.

The scoreboard can bring out a variety of emotions in all of us. Joy, disappointment, happiness, anger, excitement, anxiety, relief, and stress. The scoreboard can keep us on our toes. The scoreboard can keep our heads in the game. The scoreboard can motivate us to take our team to the next level!

—**Dale**

96

Special Needs, Special Opportunities

Do you have any special needs children in your church? I hope your answer was a resounding NO. Why? Because they're *not* "special needs children." They're children—just children. David wrote: "You made all the delicate, inner parts of my body and knit me together in my mother's womb. Thank you for making me so wonderfully complex! Your workmanship is marvelous—how well I know it" (Psalm 139:13-14).

God, in all his omnipotent wisdom and power, designed every child in your ministry exactly as they are, and he can use *all* of us to his glory, and to fulfill his plan. In our ministry, our mission begins with "To partner with parents." That means *all* parents, right? Right! Now that that's out of the way, let's talk about ministering to children who have special needs.

Let's own up to the truth: Challenges abound. It may be that God allows you to create and sustain a ministry specifically designed for these precious children. We tried that. And we failed. What we ended up with is a philosophy that has worked well—with few exceptions—for our entire culture. It's worked on multiple campuses, in multiple states, regardless of the age or size of the campus. It's called One2One. Here's how it works.

Be on the lookout.

Every member of my team is constantly on the lookout for adults who have training, experience, or a special calling for children with any variety of need.

Parents know best.

As new families visit our church and engage, we ask them to complete a short form that we use in our security system to keep their kids safe. One thing the form asks: "Does your child have any special needs we should be aware of?" If they mark yes, a team member contacts them to visit. For this most important conversation, we've taught our team members the following: "Listen, don't talk. Ask, don't answer."

We pre-screen volunteers to find one who is competent to serve a given family's specific needs. Then we arrange an introduction so they can get to know each other. During this introductory meeting, we lay out these guidelines:

A fair commitment. The family must commit to which service they will attend weekly and communicate to the volunteer if they will be absent.

Wade in gently. We set a specific trial period. We want all three parties—the parents, the volunteer, and most importantly, the child—to be comfortable with the arrangements.

Ongoing feedback. We have the parents and the volunteer agree to terms for openly communicating issues.

The parents' extra step. Parents must agree to remain constantly aware of the notification system we use in big church, and they must respond immediately if their number displays.

We outline our limitations. There have been cases where we simply were not equipped to care for a child.

If you don't know where or how to start, ask around! Whatever your church does, do it well. Respect the child. Respect the parent. And remember the words of Christ:

"I tell you the truth, when you did it to one of the least of these my brothers and sisters, you were doing it to me" (Matthew 25:40).

—Scott

97

Stop and Smell the Play-Doh!

> "For seven days you must celebrate this festival to honor the Lord your God at the place he chooses, for it is he who blesses you with bountiful harvests and gives you success in all your work. This festival will be a time of great joy for all."
>
> —Deuteronomy 16:15

God told his people to take time to slow down and remember the blessings he had given them. They were to celebrate the successes that had come from him.

I believe God wants us to slow down sometimes and remember his blessings. We need to take time to celebrate the successes he has given us in ministry.

That's not always easy to do. The pace of ministry and life in general isn't always conducive to slowing down and rejoicing in God's blessings. Family matters, weekend services, events, and meetings just keep on coming. It's hard to stop and take time to celebrate because the next weekend, event, or activity is just around the corner. In ministry, it's hard to look back at what's happened and look up to give thanks. You have to be intentional. Here are some intentional steps to help you hit "pause" in your children's ministry and rejoice in God's blessings.

Send out a weekly e-mail praise report. Each week on Monday, we e-mail a copy of the coming weekend's lesson. Part of that e-mail is sharing the blessings of the past weekend. We take time to reflect on God's blessings and the successes he has given us as a team.

Take time at each team meeting to reflect on God's blessings. Each time you meet with your volunteers, take time to share God's blessings since the last meeting.

Share stories of lives that have been touched. Regularly rejoice and celebrate the lives that have been changed. Share how you see God at work. When you get a great story of life change, send it out by e-mail to the team.

During team meetings, allow volunteers the opportunity to share how God is working in their lives and in the lives of the kids they minister to.

Take time off to reflect after big victories. As I mentioned, sometimes it's hard to take time off after a big event because another one is coming. Maybe it means going to lunch together, taking a day off work to relax and reflect, or journaling God's blessings. Do whatever it takes to pause and rejoice in God's blessings.

Create videos or picture presentations that celebrate what God has done. We have a post-camp parent meeting 30 minutes before our kids return from camp. At this meeting, we pass out a talking-points sheet so parents can talk with their kids about what they learned at camp. We also show a recap video with highlights from the week. Parents love it! We make a DVD copy of the video available for families and volunteers.

Another idea is that when kids graduate from one ministry environment to another, to make a video that reflects on their time in that ministry environment. Have a graduation party or event and show it. Make DVD copies available to families and volunteers.

Have a year-end celebration. At the end of your ministry year, take some time to celebrate what God has done. Have a party! Share highlights of the successes God has given you. Rejoice together in God's blessings!

Many of the celebration times in the Bible involved food. Have a cookout, reserve space at a restaurant, or have a picnic.

Whatever you do, make time to appreciate your ministry and those you serve with. In one of the churches where I served, there was a volunteer named Howard. Howard was a man's man. He was a retired police officer. He had been an atheist until God touched his life.

Then Howard wanted to find a way to serve the Lord, even though he was not in the best of health. He had a sweet computer system at home, and it became his way to make a difference. He made all the fliers, brochures, and handouts for our children's ministry. I spent many hours at Howard's house working on these things with him. We became good friends.

We also had the same favorite football team...the Dallas Cowboys. Howard had an awesome picture plaque by his computer of the '93 Cowboys who won the Super Bowl. I told him how cool it was, and we often talked about how things were going for the Cowboys.

One day Howard's wife, Mary, called me in a panic. Howard had passed out and fallen out of his computer chair. I immediately rushed to the house and got there just as the paramedics were arriving. Howard was lying on his back unconscious. I held Mary's hand as the paramedics worked to revive him. Howard never regained consciousness. He was gone. God had called him home.

After the funeral, Mary brought me the Cowboys plaque from Howard's office. She said, "Howard loved you. He would want you to have this." It's been hanging in my office ever since. I often pause to look at it, remember Howard, and reflect on the wonderful times we had serving together.

The time God has given you to minister is precious. Don't rush through it without pausing to reflect on and rejoice in your blessings. Make sure you take time to celebrate the successes.

Stop and smell the Play-Doh!

—**Dale**

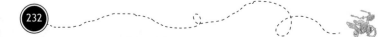

98

Coaching and Counseling

For years I struggled with communication issues in certain meeting situations at church. I'm passionate. Ironically, the very passion that often propelled us forward was the same passion that got me in trouble. If my boss said it once, he said it a million times: "It's not the message. It's the delivery." Time after time, I felt misunderstood. Or I unintentionally hurt someone's feelings. Or I simply steamrolled someone in a meeting. I didn't mean to. I didn't want to. I just didn't feel like we had time to walk on eggshells to protect everyone else's fragile feelings. I figured, *I can take it. Why can't they?*

After one such exchange, I was asked...no, *strongly encouraged...*to "spend some time with Bill." My supervisors said, "He's a great communications coach. He can help." I didn't need help. All these stained-glass people did. I wasn't crazy about the idea, because I had always thought something had to be wrong with you for you to go with counseling. And that's just what I needed to face.

Something *was* wrong.

Seek wise counsel.

Who goes to counseling? Messed-up people, right? That's not what Proverbs 11:14 says: "Without wise leadership, a nation falls; there is safety in having many advisers."

"Bill" is a business executive and an educated counselor. My leadership was right. Bill offered exactly what I needed. He didn't solve all my problems. He didn't show me how to change the world. Just mine. As I began opening up to his counsel, I found myself finally able to actually *listen* to what I was saying, *and how I was saying it.* I was shocked, even appalled. I needed to change. That was almost two years ago, and with few exceptions I've met with Bill every week since. Ours is a relationship I cherish, one I wouldn't want to be without. Bill offers me an unbiased outlet for my frustrations, successful strategies for my challenges and shortcomings, and insight into aspects of myself that I previously never even knew existed.

Admit the truth: You need help.

Jesus said the truth sets us free. And it's the only thing that does. The truth is, if you answer the call to minister to God's precious children, there will be many times, and maybe many areas, where you're going to need help. And that's OK. Where do you start?

Start with God.

Pray. Ask God for his help and guidance. According to Scripture, he has great plans for you—plans to bless you and not to harm you. Ask him to reveal areas of weakness and to provide you with a way of escape.

Seek leadership insight.

Talk to people God has placed in authority over you. Many times, those leading you can identify areas in you which could be refined (maybe even totally renovated). Ask them to help you define those areas from their perspective. But when you ask, be ready for the answer. Guard your heart.

Prioritize.

Once you've determined what areas you need to address, prioritize. Which areas seem to be holding you back the most? Which areas are keeping you from being most effective? Which areas are constraining God's very best in your life and ministry?

Take baby steps.

In the movie *What About Bob?* one of the characters writes a "groundbreaking new book," *Baby Steps.* Take small steps, and keep going. Nothing changes overnight. That's OK. Make small adjustments every day. Over time, you'll look up and realize you're heading in a new direction. Guess what? Others will see it, too!

Throughout my time with Bill, my wife and my boss have had a running joke. I call what Bill does coaching (that sounds less damaged). My boss calls it counseling. My wife calls it anger management. It's all three. I'm not perfect. I never will be. But I'm better.

And now I can say, without any hesitation, "Yes, I go to counseling! You mean you don't?"

—Scott

99

When Kids Pray

It's awesome to hear kids pray. You can hear their simple faith and feel their sincerity as they reach toward God.

Everything in this book is of no avail without prayer. Nothing of eternal value will be accomplished without it. Whatever you do, teach kids to pray. Give them opportunity to pray. And when they pray, you will see God move.

Let me tell you a story.

In the early '90s, I served at a new church plant in California. Being a new church, we didn't have a lot of money for salaries, so we had to rent a house in a neighborhood that was less than desirable. A few doors down lived the meanest man in the neighborhood. He was an ex-gang member and had a history of violence and criminal activities such as drug dealing. I went down to invite him to church, and he quickly told me that he had never been to church, was an atheist, and wanted no part of God. I invited him several times, but to no avail.

A few months later, I noticed two boys walking by my house. I stopped them and invited them to church. One was in fourth grade and one was in fifth grade. They said they had never been to church but would like to go. I told them we would need their parents' permission if they wanted to go. I asked who their father was, and guess where they pointed...you got it...the ex-gang member. *Oh boy...here we go. He'll probably say no, but let's give it a try.* To my surprise, he said the boys could go if they wanted to, but he quickly reminded me that he personally wanted no part of church or God.

The boys began attending church with our family. We would drive down and pick them up every Sunday morning. After several months, they both stepped across the line of faith and became Christ-followers. We began to pray together for their parents to step across the line of faith as well.

One day after class I was cleaning up and noticed a piece of paper on the floor. The boys' class had written out prayer requests that day on slips of paper. This piece of paper was the neighbor boys' prayer request slip. It simply read "We prayed seven times this week that our father would accept Jesus into his life."

I stuck the paper in my pocket and when I dropped the boys off, I handed it to their father. I said, "You might want to read this." He had been drinking heavily that day. He grabbed the paper out of my hand, mumbled something, and stumbled back in the house.

The next weekend I went to pick up the boys. Normally they ran out to the car, but this time the door didn't open. I went up and knocked. One of the boys stuck his head out the door and said they wouldn't be riding with me. My heart sank. I must have made their father so mad that he wasn't going to let them come anymore. But then the boy went on. He said, "We're going to ride with our father today!" I couldn't believe it!

Their father walked in church that Sunday for the first time. We had an L.A. County sheriff who was familiar with his past criminal history. The sheriff approached us and said he would be watching the man carefully in case he tried to steal something.

I was leading the children's worship that day for grades 1-3. After the service, those two boys came running to me. They were yelling out, "Dad accepted Christ! Dad accepted Christ!" Their father had walked forward and given his life to Christ at the end of the service! My heart exploded with joy! We hugged, cried, and jumped up and down!

Their mother also gave her life to Christ a short time later. Their father went on to become a minister and has personally brought hundreds of people to Christ. I talked to him just a few weeks ago, and he is still passionately following Christ.

Prayer made all the difference in that family's life, and it can do the same for families you know!

—**Dale**

My pastor is phenomenal at keeping present in the minds of our staff and our church body who we are, what we stand for, and even why we're a church. At every all-staff meeting, at every membership class, and with every communication, he either refers to our mission or recites it verbatim.

He also consistently communicates our action steps and our core values. I'm going to share them with you here. I hope that reading them inspires you to either establish this practice within your ministry or to renew your commitment to it.

- *Mission.* To lead people to become fully devoted followers of Christ.

- *Purpose.* Bring in, build up, train, send out.

- *Core Values.* (SPECIES) Sacrifice, Passion, Excellence, Community, Integrity, Evangelism, Stewardship.

Live who you are. If your church doesn't have stated values—a mission statement, a list of core values, or some written guiding ideas like those—talk to your senior pastor about it. If your team and church body don't know who they are, they won't be willing to give their all to the church's vision. If you *do* have value statements established, incorporate them into your daily decisions, your team interactions, and your volunteer-training sessions. As a unified team with a common language and common goals, you'll be able to accomplish more, and you'll experience greater unity.

Catch (and share) a vision just for your kids. Using the mission and core values that leadership provided as a foundation, our team further tailored them for our specific ministry. Here they are:

- *Mission.* To partner with parents in providing their children with the skills, experiences, and resources that will lead them to become fully devoted followers of Christ.

- *Directional statements.* To...

…create an experience for children from newborns through fifth grade that encourages learning.

…provide an experience for children that encourages their desire to attend and return.

…stimulate children's minds through their surroundings.

…explore children's imaginations through creative thought and teaching methods.

…interact with children and have fun through activities and games.

…teach children the truths of God's Word in relevant, age-appropriate fashion.

Incorporate specific core values for your specific ministry. Besides our church's seven core values, we incorporated these additional core values and descriptions into all our training:

- *Evangelism.* (Matthew 28:19-20) Through cultural relevance and bold methods, we purposefully expose the children of LifeChurch.tv to the truth of God's Word.

- *Excellence.* (Colossians 3:17) Attention to detail honors God and inspires people.

- *Sacrifice.* (Matthew 10:39) Through our time and resources, we give up something we value for something of even more value.

- *Passion.* (Romans 1:16) We model the life of a fully devoted follower of Christ to the children entrusted into our care. We lead them with excitement, enthusiasm, and joy.

- *Consistency.* (Colossians 3:17) We continually strive to provide continuity in our approach to ministry and its implementation within LifeChurch.tv.

- *Submission to Authority.* (Hebrews 13:17) As a ministry, we operate fully under the authority and leadership of the triad God, his Word, and the leadership of LifeChurch.tv.

- *Relationship.* (Ecclesiastes 4:12) Through intentional programming, we facilitate relationship between the children of LifeChurch.tv to build a support network that transcends the church and invades their lives.

- *Creativity.* (Psalm 40:3) We will strive to hear a fresh word from the Lord in ministry and its components. We will trust in the voice and leadership of the Holy Spirit to speak, and we will follow with 100 percent obedience to his voice.

- *Safety.* (Psalm 91:11) Realizing the enormity of being entrusted with the safety, instruction, and care of children, we will cover our areas in prayer, and we will practice due diligence through the procedures in place to ensure their safety in every way.

- *Empowerment.* (2 Timothy 2:2) Realizing that God has equipped the body for his service, we will constantly strive to utilize those gifts throughout our ministry, ensuring that we maintain the level of excellence the vision mandates.

- *Trust.* (Matthew 5:37) We will always choose to give those in our ministry the benefit of the doubt, restoring those who fall and are repentant, while trusting in God's sovereign protection.

By holding God's Word in its proper place as the scriptural basis for our values, we embrace it in our daily decisions. Our Bible-based vision became the fabric, the very language, that represents our ministry. It can do the same for you!

—**Scott**

Dale Hudson has served in Children's Ministry for over 23 years. He is the Director of Children's Ministry at Christ Fellowship Church in South Florida. Dale was voted one of the 20 Most Influential Voices in Children's Ministry. His website, relevantchildrensministry.com, provides ideas, insight, and content for leaders. Dale and his wife, Pamela, have been married for 23 years and have two sons: Josh, who is 22, and Caleb, who is 18.

Scott Werner is a husband and father of three sons and resides with his family in Edmond, Oklahoma. He was blessed to serve as the Executive Director of Children's Ministries at his home church, LifeChurch.tv, from 2002 to 2007. During his tenure with Life, the ministry grew from two campuses to 12, with more than 40 weekend worship experiences. Attendance for children (ages birth through 12) grew from about 800 per weekend to more than 5,000.

Scott led a team of 30 full-time paid staff, 100 part-time staff, and over 1,000 weekly volunteers. He has also led numerous special events, including summer camps and the turbocharged VBX, with over 2,000 children in attendance each day. Following his time at Life, he served for 4 years with Compassion International, ministering to children worldwide. His greatest passion is to empower children and partner with parents in leading their children to live their lives as fully devoted followers of Christ. Currently, Scott and Tammy are continuing to minister to families in their home community as the operating partners of My Small Wonders, a private faith-based child development center.